CAPTAIN AMERICA®

HAIL HYDRA!

D0413025

WRITER: JONATHAN MABERRY
ARTISTS: SERGIO CARIELLO, TOM SCIOLI, PHIL WINSLADE, KYLE HOTZ & GRAHAM NOLAN

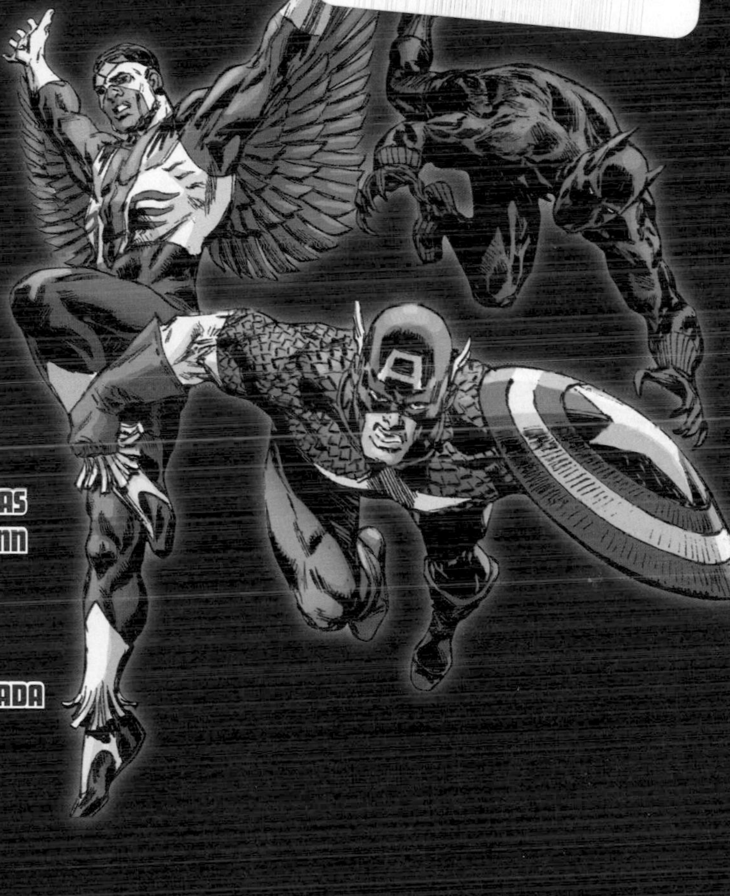

COLOURS: CHRIS SOTOMAYER, BILL CRABTREE WITH SOTO, CHRIS CHUCKRY, DAN BROWN & IAN HANNIN
LETTERS: VC'S JOE CARAMAGNA, CLAYTON COWLES & JOE SABINO
ASSISTNAT EDITOR: RACHEL PINNELAS
CONSULTING EDITOR: BILL ROSEMANN
EDITOR: TOM BRENNAN
EDITOR IN CHIEF: AXEL ALONSO

CHIEF CREATIVE OFFICER: JOE QUESADA
PUBLISHER: DAN BUCKLEY
EXECUTIVE PRODUCER: ALAN FINE

COVER ART: ADI GRANOV

Do you have any comments or queries about this graphic novel? Email us at graphicnovels@panini.co.uk

CAPTAIN AMERICA: HAIL HYDRA. Contains material originally published in magazine form as CAPTAIN AMERICA: HAIL HYDRA #1-5. First printing 2011. Published by Panini Publishing, a division of Panini UK Limited. Mike Riddell, Managing Director. Alan O'Keefe, Managing Editor. Mark Irvine, Production Manager. Marco M. Lupoi, Publishing Director Europe. Brady Webb, Reprint Editor. Angela Hart, Designer. Office of publication: Brockbourne House, 77 Mount Ephraim, Tunbridge Wells, Kent TN4 8BS.
Printed in Italy. ISBN: 978-1-84653-488-1

MARVEL GRAPHIC NOVEL CAPTAIN AMERICA: HAIL HYDRA #1

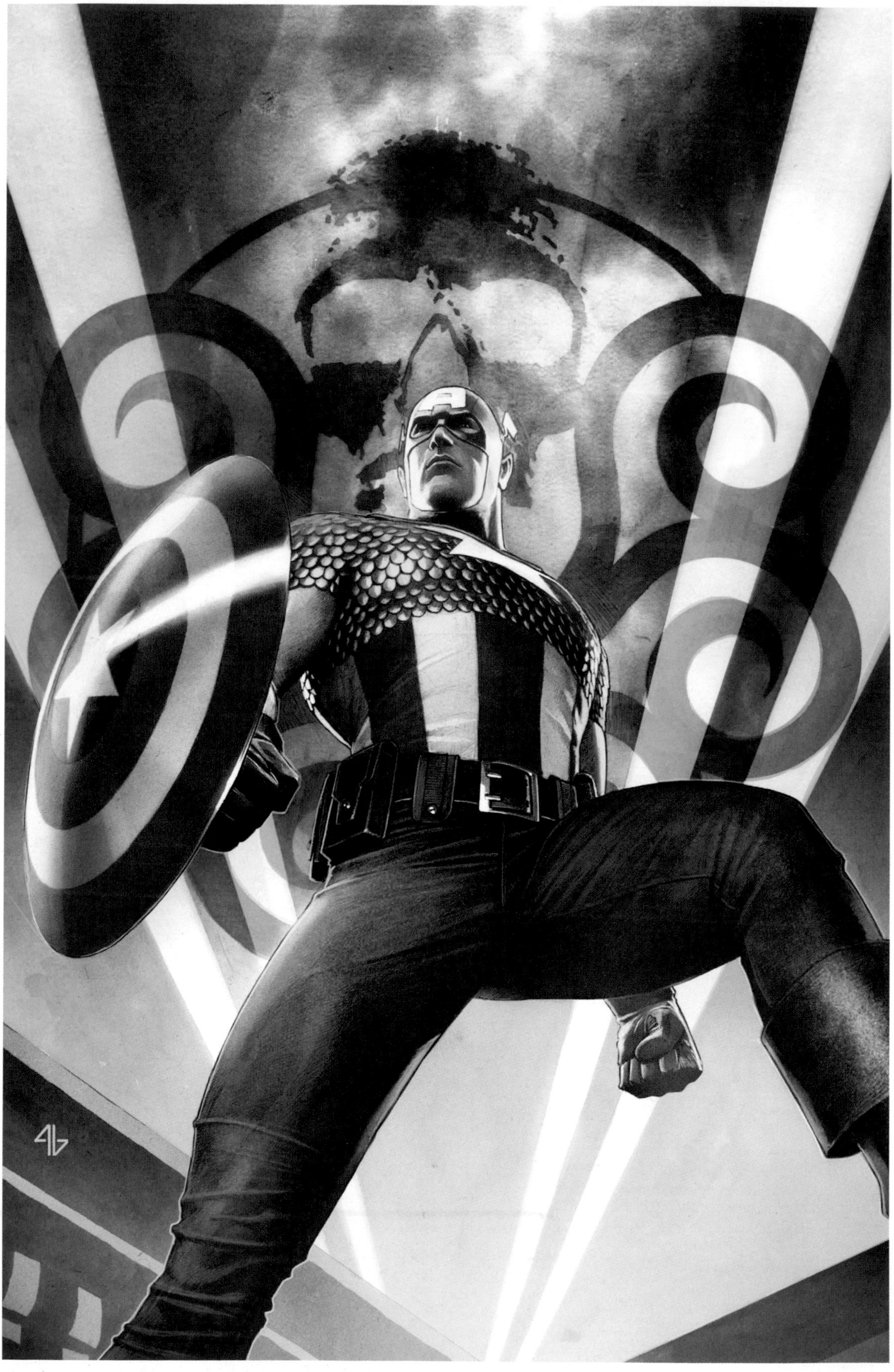

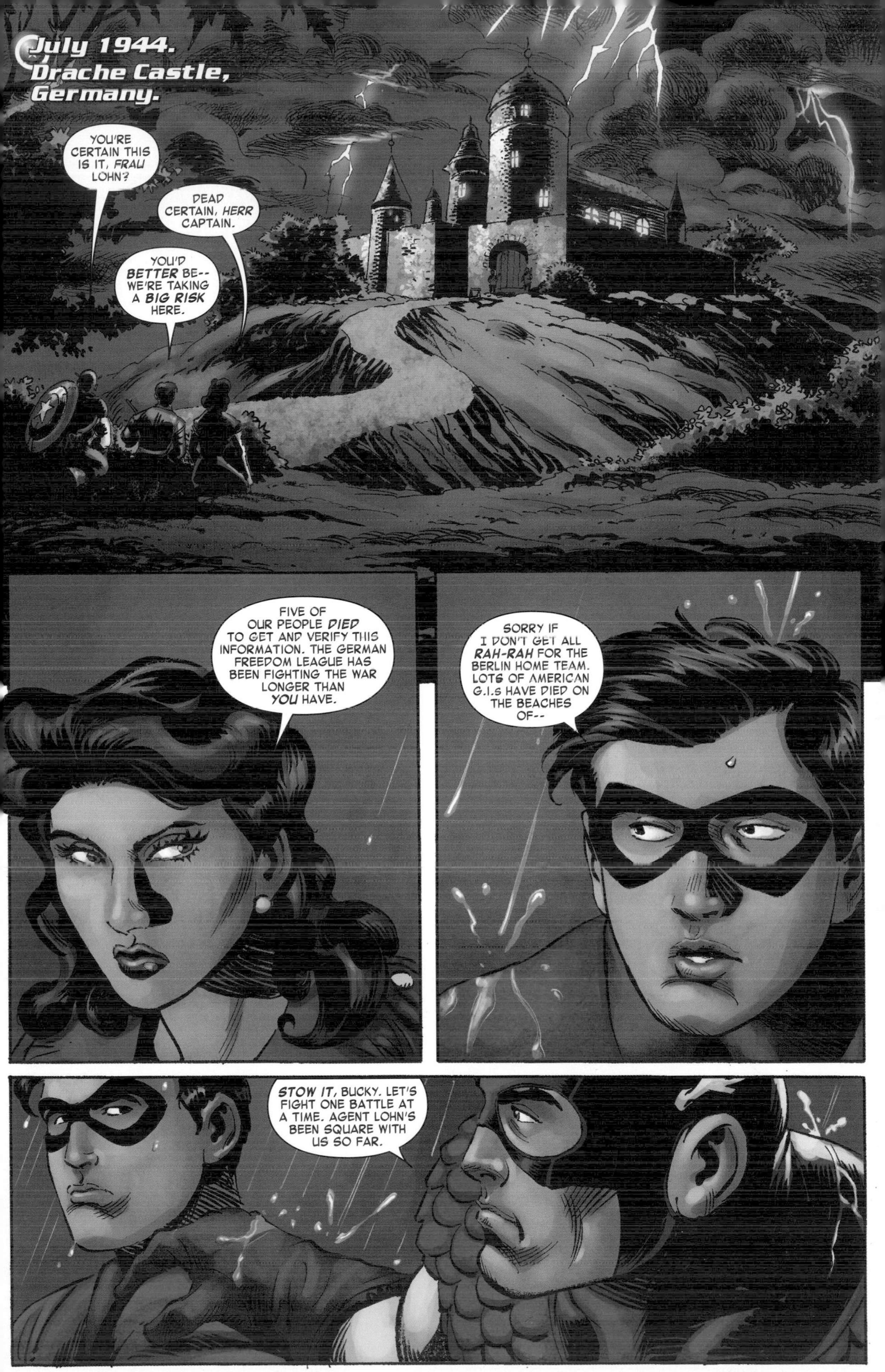
July 1944. Drache Castle, Germany.
YOU'RE CERTAIN THIS IS IT, FRAU LOHN?
DEAD CERTAIN, HERR CAPTAIN.
YOU'D BETTER BE-- WE'RE TAKING A BIG RISK HERE.
FIVE OF OUR PEOPLE DIED TO GET AND VERIFY THIS INFORMATION. THE GERMAN FREEDOM LEAGUE HAS BEEN FIGHTING THE WAR LONGER THAN YOU HAVE.
SORRY IF I DON'T GET ALL RAH-RAH FOR THE BERLIN HOME TEAM. LOTS OF AMERICAN G.I.s HAVE DIED ON THE BEACHES OF--
STOW IT, BUCKY. LET'S FIGHT ONE BATTLE AT A TIME. AGENT LOHN'S BEEN SQUARE WITH US SO FAR.

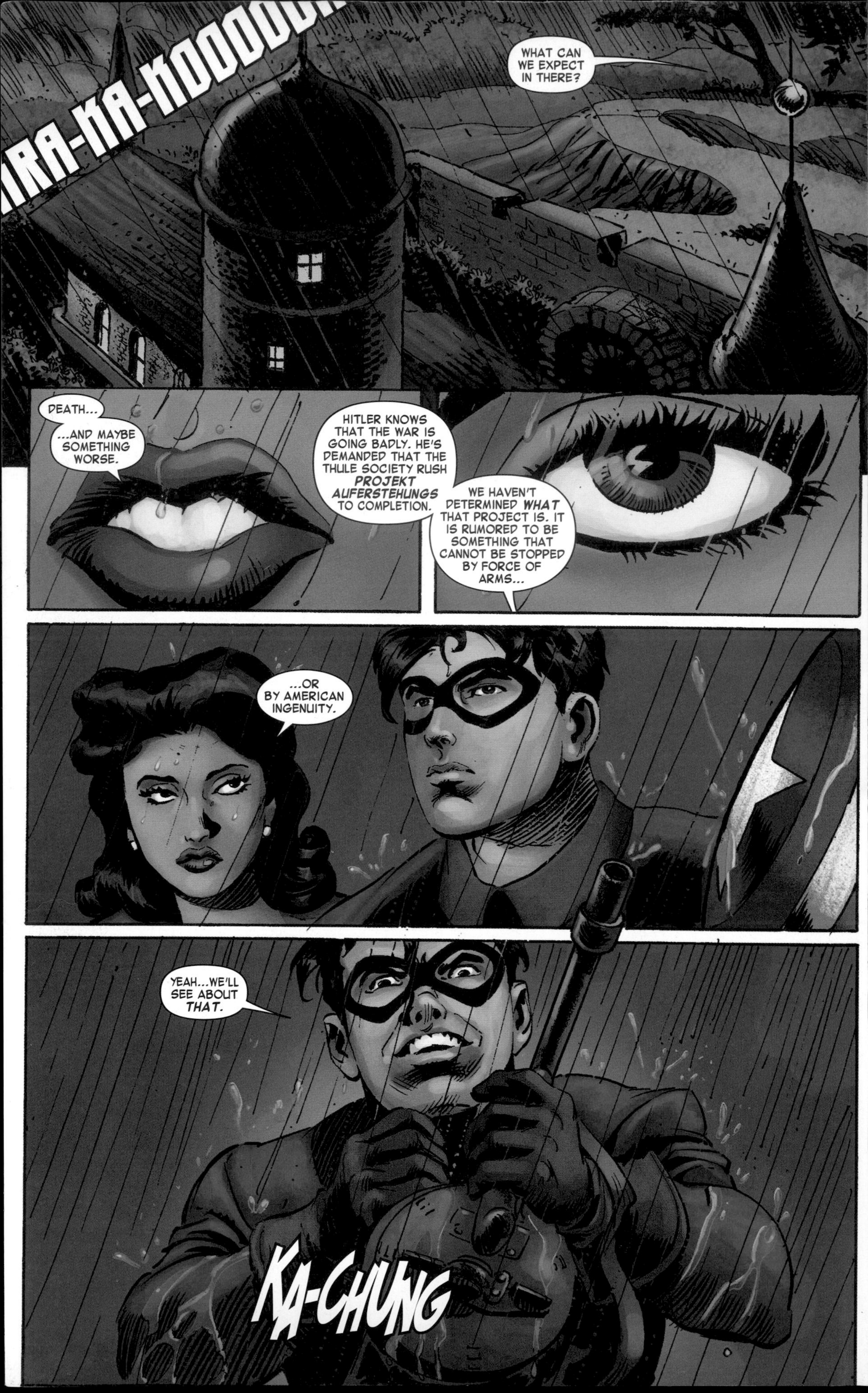
KRA-KA-KOOOOOM!
WHAT CAN WE EXPECT IN THERE?
DEATH...
...AND MAYBE SOMETHING WORSE.
HITLER KNOWS THAT THE WAR IS GOING BADLY. HE'S DEMANDED THAT THE THULE SOCIETY RUSH *PROJEKT AUFERSTEHUNGS* TO COMPLETION.
WE HAVEN'T DETERMINED *WHAT* THAT PROJECT IS. IT IS RUMORED TO BE SOMETHING THAT CANNOT BE STOPPED BY FORCE OF ARMS...
...OR BY AMERICAN INGENUITY.
YEAH...WE'LL SEE ABOUT *THAT.*
KA-CHUNG

"THE THULES ARE THE LATEST INCARNATION OF AN ANCIENT SOCIETY OF SCIENTIST MYSTICS.

"THEY ARE UTTERLY RUTHLESS-- AND TOTALLY DEDICATED TO THE BELIEF IN THE MASTER RACE IDEAL. ANYONE WHO DOESN'T FIT IS *LEBENSUNWERTES LEBEN.*

"'LIFE UNWORTHY OF LIFE.'

"ONLY SOLDIERS EQUALLY RUTHLESS AND COMMITTED STAND A CHANCE AGAINST THEM.

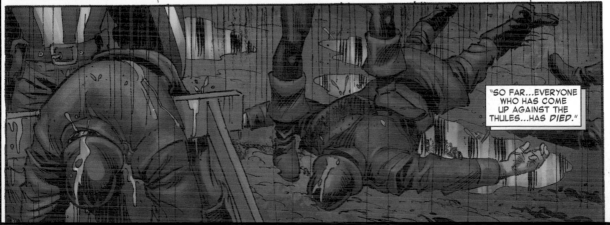

"SO FAR...EVERYONE WHO HAS COME UP AGAINST THE THULES...HAS *DIED.*"

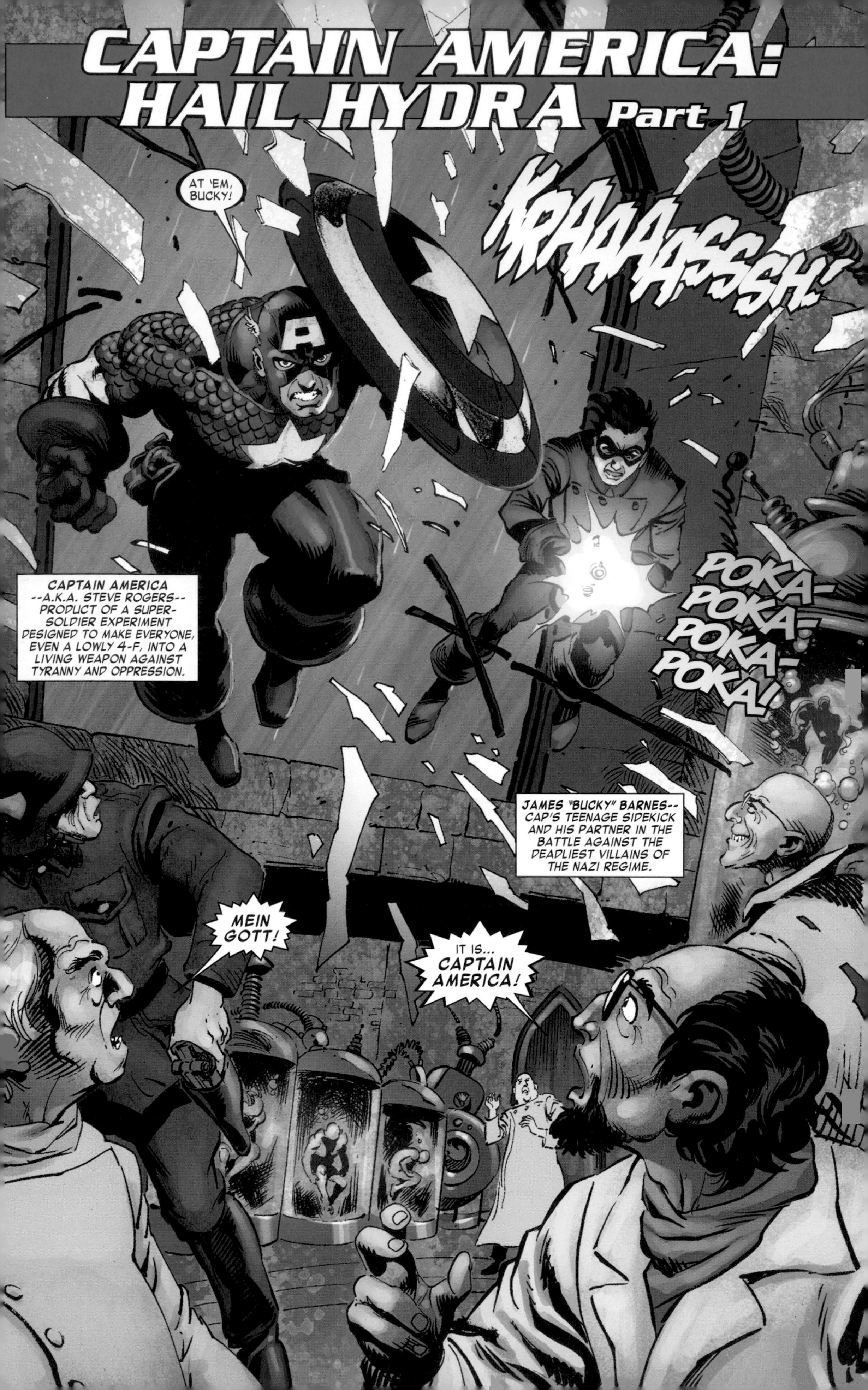
CAPTAIN AMERICA: HAIL HYDRA Part 1
AT 'EM, BUCKY!
KRAAAASSSH!
CAPTAIN AMERICA --A.K.A. STEVE ROGERS-- PRODUCT OF A SUPER-SOLDIER EXPERIMENT DESIGNED TO MAKE EVERYONE, EVEN A LOWLY 4-F, INTO A LIVING WEAPON AGAINST TYRANNY AND OPPRESSION.
POKA-POKA-POKA-POKA!
JAMES "BUCKY" BARNES-- CAP'S TEENAGE SIDEKICK AND HIS PARTNER IN THE BATTLE AGAINST THE DEADLIEST VILLAINS OF THE NAZI REGIME.
MEIN GOTT!
IT IS... CAPTAIN AMERICA!

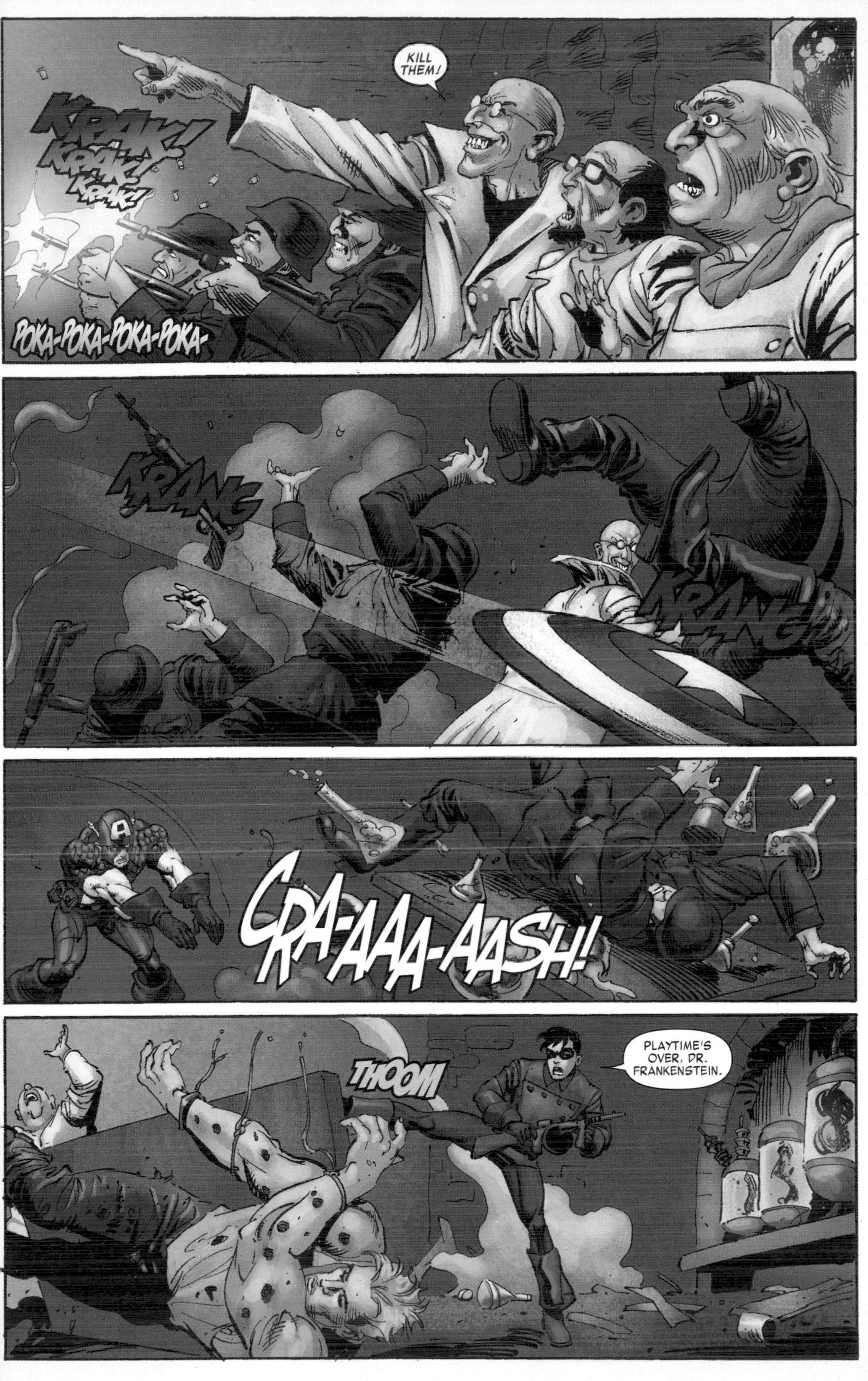
KILL THEM!
KRAK! KRAK! KRAK!
POKA-POKA-POKA-POKA-
KRANG
KRANG
CRA-AAA-AASH!
THOOM
PLAYTIME'S OVER, DR. FRANKENSTEIN.

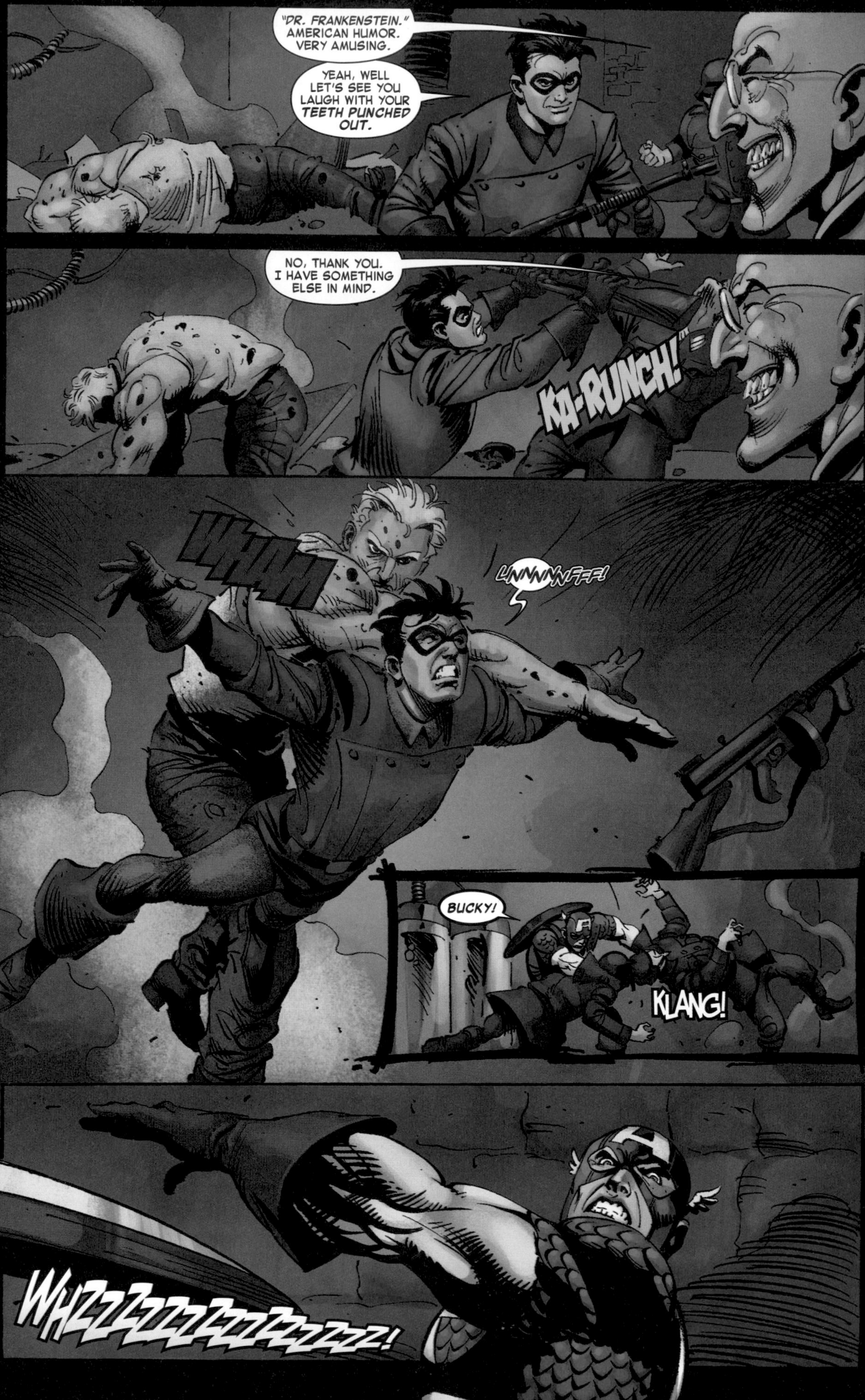
"DR. FRANKENSTEIN." AMERICAN HUMOR. VERY AMUSING.
YEAH, WELL LET'S SEE YOU LAUGH WITH YOUR TEETH PUNCHED OUT.
NO, THANK YOU. I HAVE SOMETHING ELSE IN MIND.
KA-RUNCH!
WHAM
UNNNNNFFF!
BUCKY!
KLANG!
WHZZZZZZZZZZZZZZZZ!

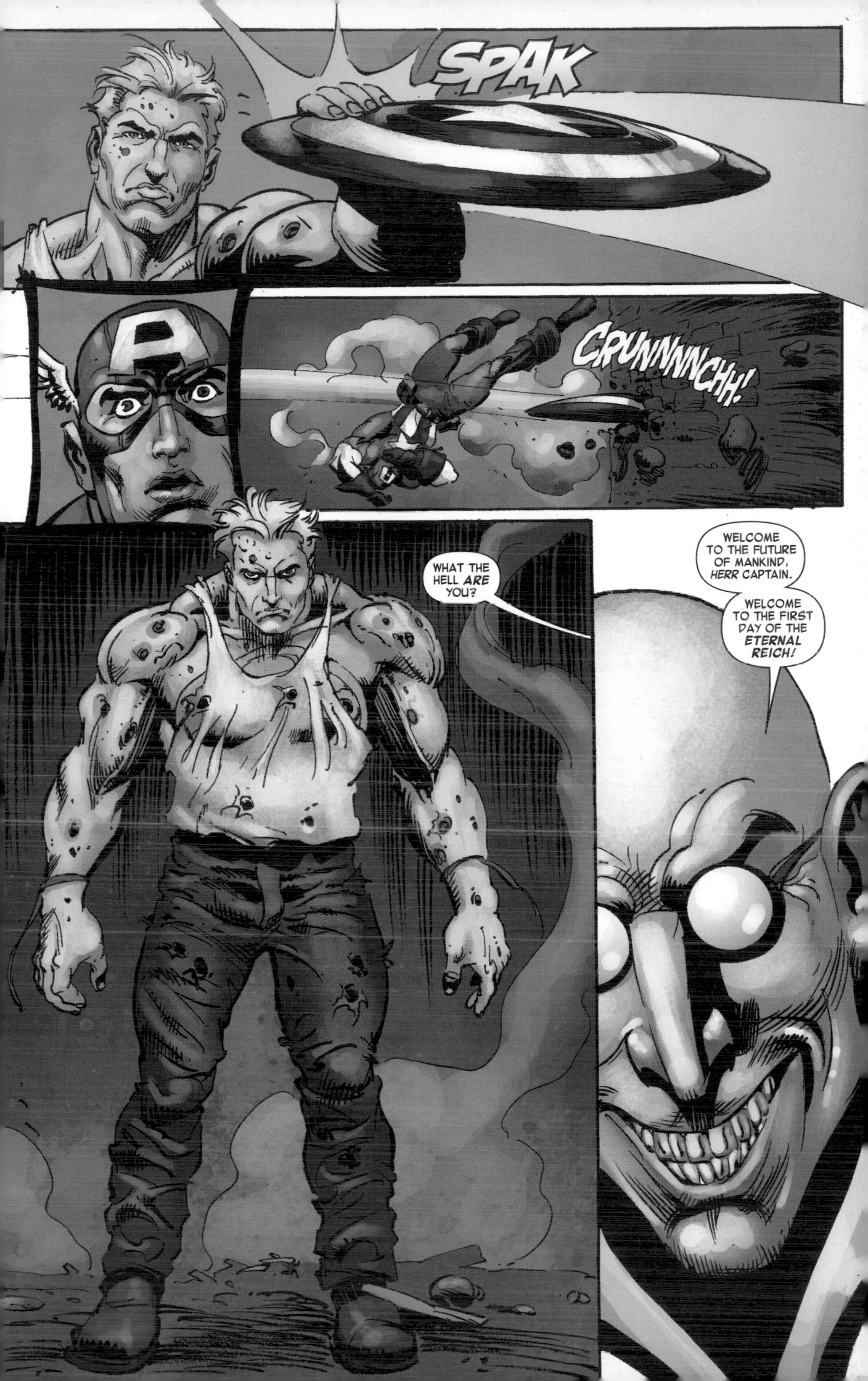
SPAK
CRUNNNNCHH!
WHAT THE HELL ARE YOU?
WELCOME TO THE FUTURE OF MANKIND, HERR CAPTAIN.
WELCOME TO THE FIRST DAY OF THE ETERNAL REICH!

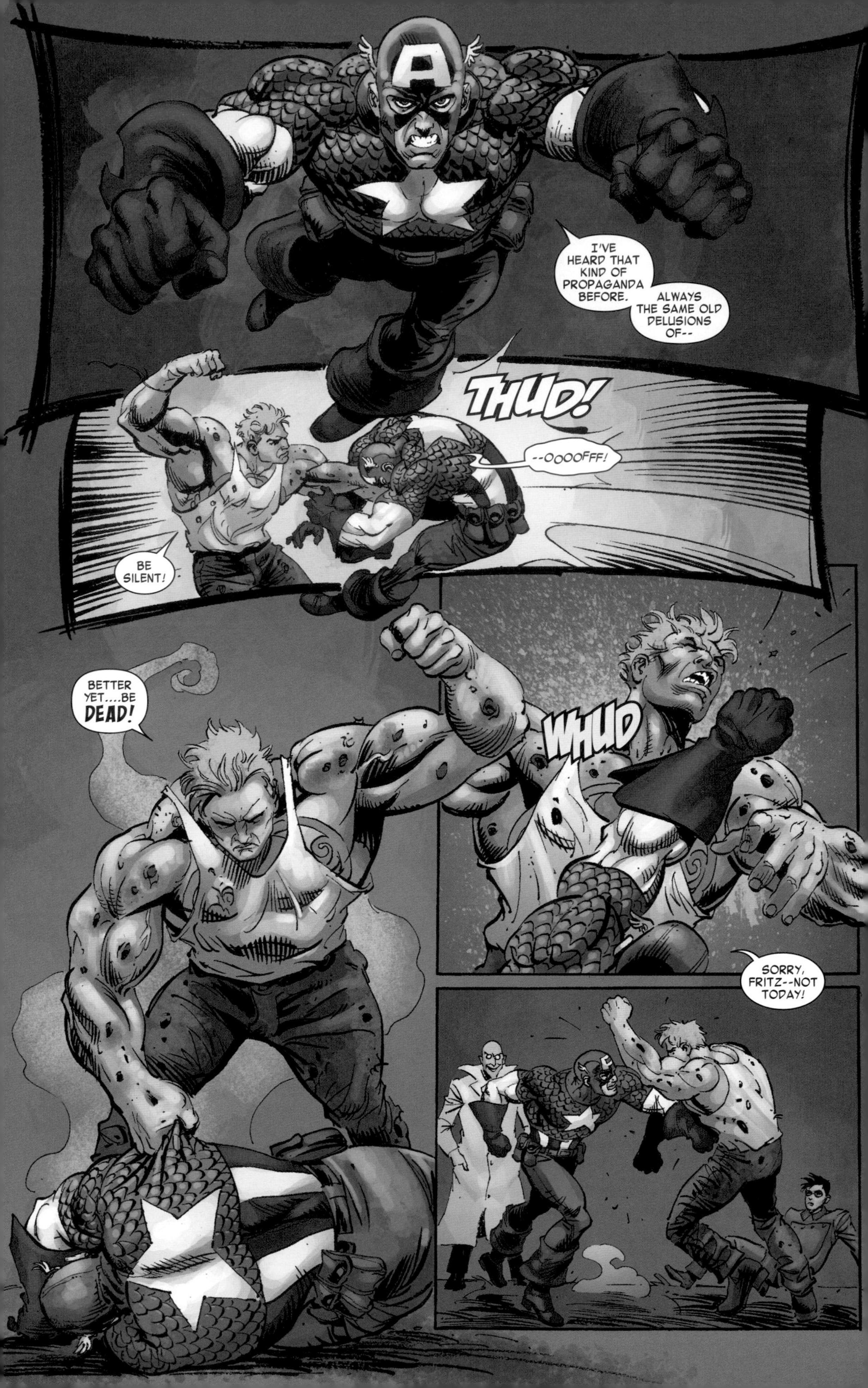
I'VE HEARD THAT KIND OF PROPAGANDA BEFORE.
ALWAYS THE SAME OLD DELUSIONS OF--
THUD!
--OOOOFFF!
BE SILENT!
BETTER YET....BE DEAD!
WHUD
SORRY, FRITZ--NOT TODAY!

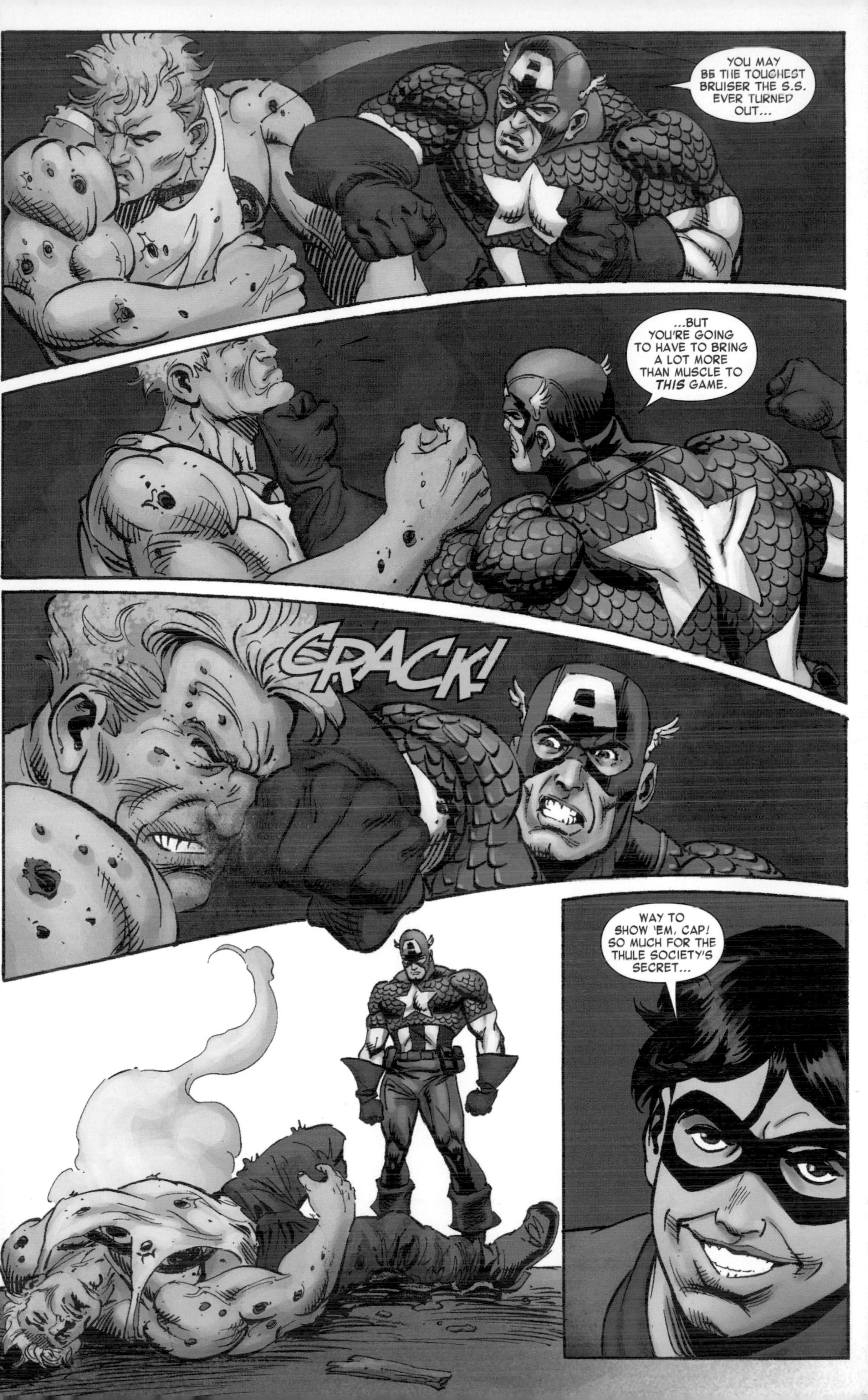
YOU MAY BE THE TOUGHEST BRUISER THE S.S. EVER TURNED OUT...
...BUT YOU'RE GOING TO HAVE TO BRING A LOT MORE THAN MUSCLE TO *THIS* GAME.
CRACK!
WAY TO SHOW 'EM, CAP! SO MUCH FOR THE THULE SOCIETY'S SECRET...

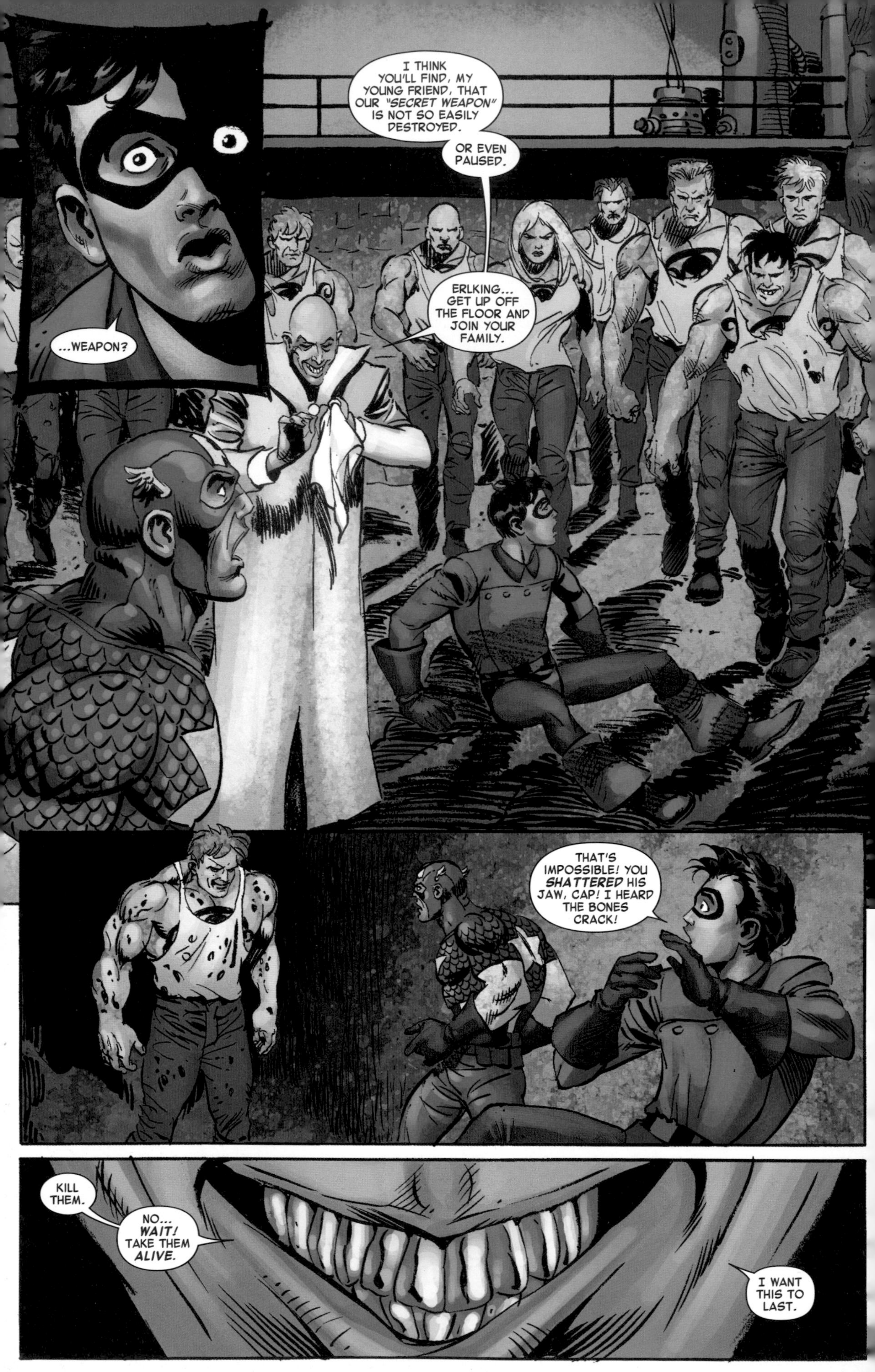
...WEAPON?
I THINK YOU'LL FIND, MY YOUNG FRIEND, THAT OUR "SECRET WEAPON" IS NOT SO EASILY DESTROYED.
OR EVEN PAUSED.
ERLKING... GET UP OFF THE FLOOR AND JOIN YOUR FAMILY.
THAT'S IMPOSSIBLE! YOU SHATTERED HIS JAW, CAP! I HEARD THE BONES CRACK!
KILL THEM.
NO... WAIT! TAKE THEM ALIVE.
I WANT THIS TO LAST.

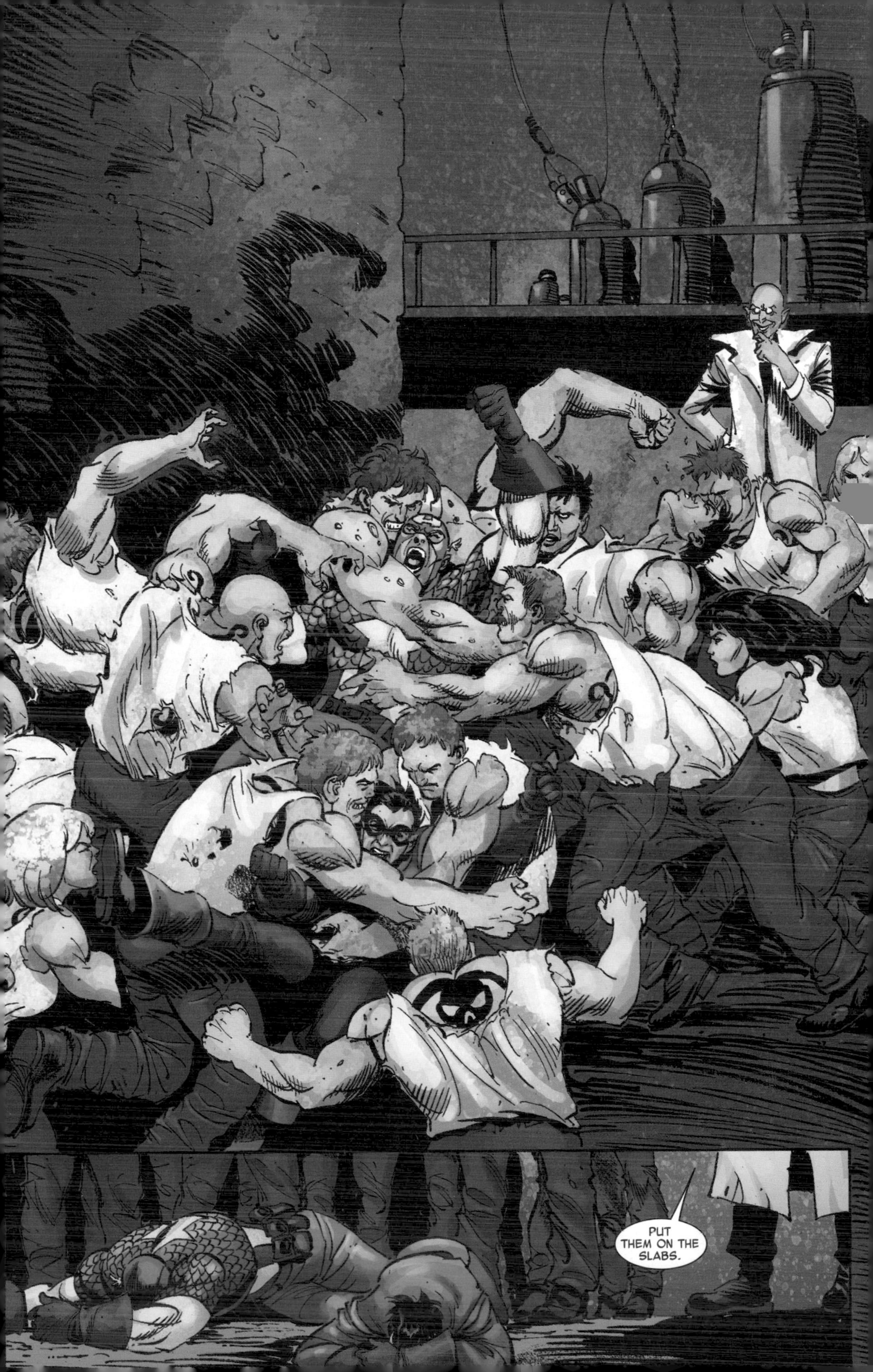
PUT THEM ON THE SLABS.

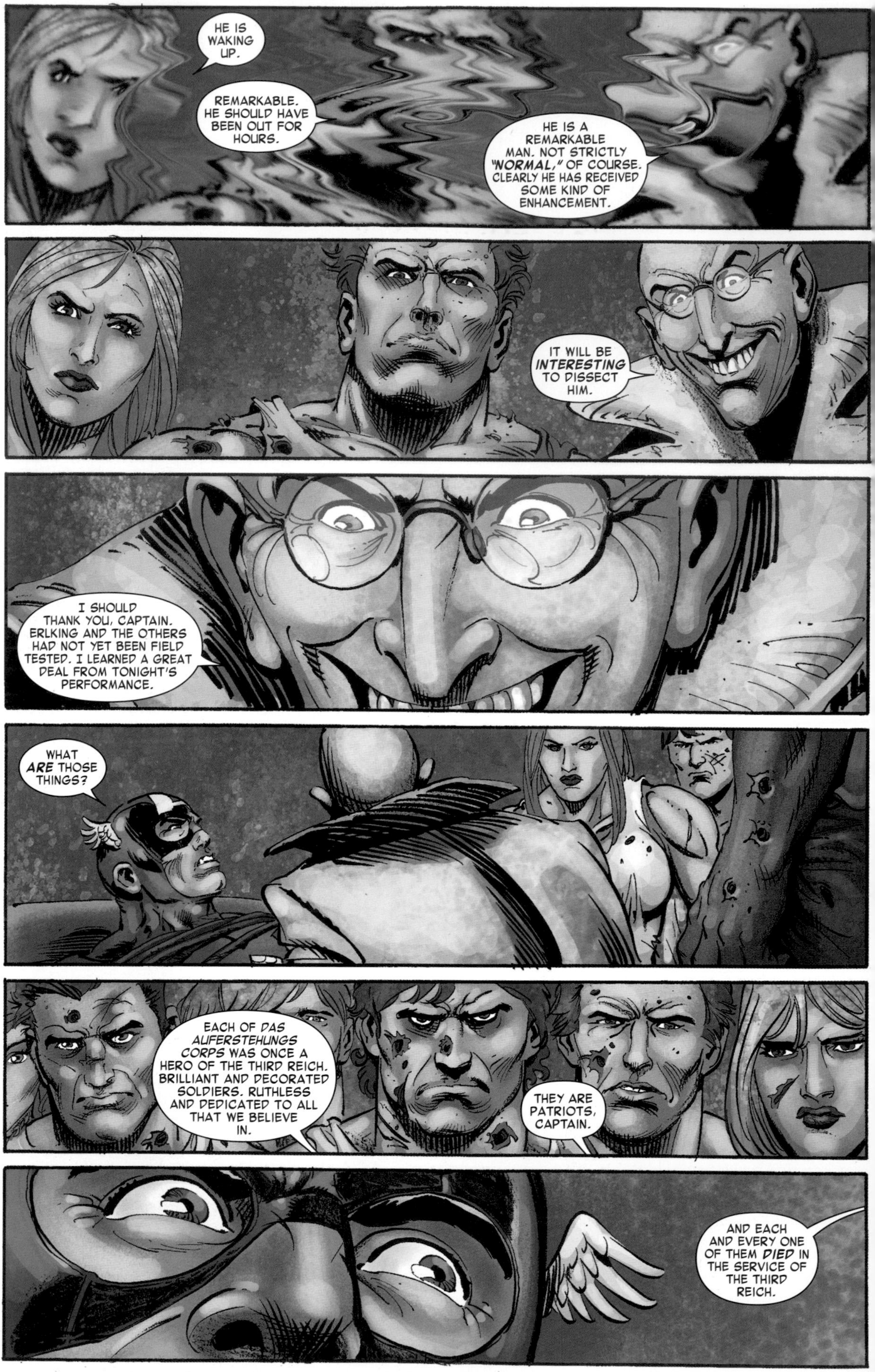
HE IS WAKING UP.
REMARKABLE. HE SHOULD HAVE BEEN OUT FOR HOURS.
HE IS A REMARKABLE MAN. NOT STRICTLY "NORMAL," OF COURSE. CLEARLY HE HAS RECEIVED SOME KIND OF ENHANCEMENT.
IT WILL BE INTERESTING TO DISSECT HIM.
I SHOULD THANK YOU, CAPTAIN. ERLKING AND THE OTHERS HAD NOT YET BEEN FIELD TESTED. I LEARNED A GREAT DEAL FROM TONIGHT'S PERFORMANCE.
WHAT ARE THOSE THINGS?
EACH OF DAS AUFERSTEHUNGS CORPS WAS ONCE A HERO OF THE THIRD REICH. BRILLIANT AND DECORATED SOLDIERS. RUTHLESS AND DEDICATED TO ALL THAT WE BELIEVE IN.
THEY ARE PATRIOTS, CAPTAIN.
AND EACH AND EVERY ONE OF THEM DIED IN THE SERVICE OF THE THIRD REICH.

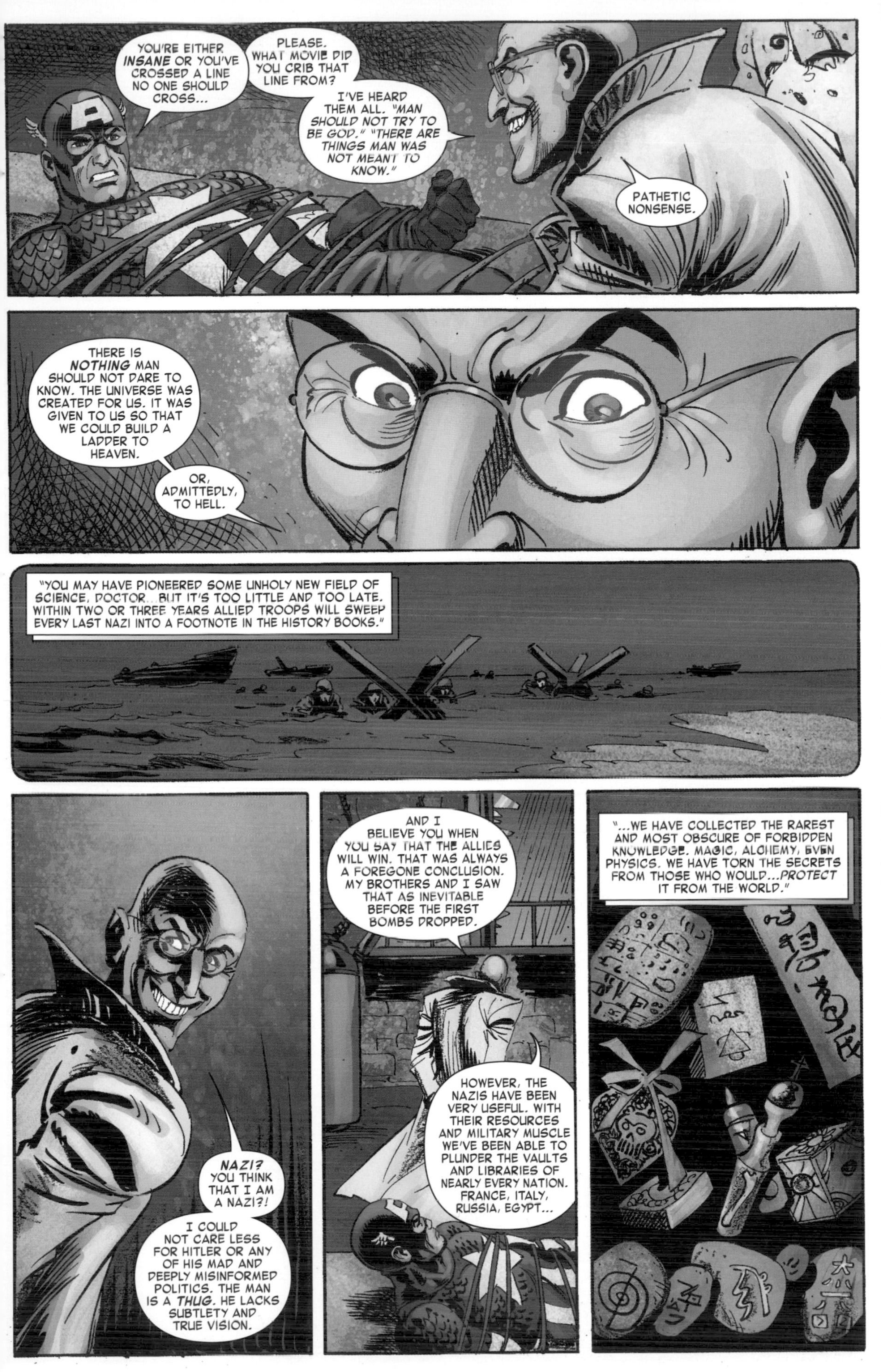
YOU'RE EITHER *INSANE* OR YOU'VE CROSSED A LINE NO ONE SHOULD CROSS...
PLEASE. WHAT MOVIE DID YOU CRIB THAT LINE FROM?
I'VE HEARD THEM ALL. *"MAN SHOULD NOT TRY TO BE GOD." "THERE ARE THINGS MAN WAS NOT MEANT TO KNOW."*
PATHETIC NONSENSE.
THERE IS *NOTHING* MAN SHOULD NOT DARE TO KNOW. THE UNIVERSE WAS CREATED FOR US. IT WAS GIVEN TO US SO THAT WE COULD BUILD A LADDER TO HEAVEN.
OR, ADMITTEDLY, TO HELL.
"YOU MAY HAVE PIONEERED SOME UNHOLY NEW FIELD OF SCIENCE, DOCTOR... BUT IT'S TOO LITTLE AND TOO LATE. WITHIN TWO OR THREE YEARS ALLIED TROOPS WILL SWEEP EVERY LAST NAZI INTO A FOOTNOTE IN THE HISTORY BOOKS."
NAZI? YOU THINK THAT I AM A NAZI?!
I COULD NOT CARE LESS FOR HITLER OR ANY OF HIS MAD AND DEEPLY MISINFORMED POLITICS. THE MAN IS A *THUG.* HE LACKS SUBTLETY AND TRUE VISION.
AND I BELIEVE YOU WHEN YOU SAY THAT THE ALLIES WILL WIN. THAT WAS ALWAYS A FOREGONE CONCLUSION. MY BROTHERS AND I SAW THAT AS INEVITABLE BEFORE THE FIRST BOMBS DROPPED.
HOWEVER, THE NAZIS HAVE BEEN VERY USEFUL. WITH THEIR RESOURCES AND MILITARY MUSCLE WE'VE BEEN ABLE TO PLUNDER THE VAULTS AND LIBRARIES OF NEARLY EVERY NATION. FRANCE, ITALY, RUSSIA, EGYPT...
"...WE HAVE COLLECTED THE RAREST AND MOST OBSCURE OF FORBIDDEN KNOWLEDGE. MAGIC, ALCHEMY, EVEN PHYSICS. WE HAVE TORN THE SECRETS FROM THOSE WHO WOULD...*PROTECT* IT FROM THE WORLD."

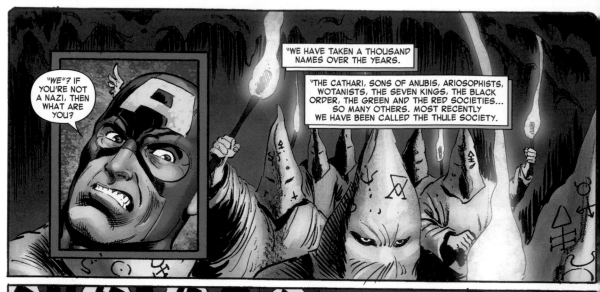

"WE HAVE TAKEN A THOUSAND NAMES OVER THE YEARS.

"THE CATHARI, SONS OF ANUBIS, ARIOSOPHISTS, WOTANISTS, THE SEVEN KINGS, THE BLACK ORDER, THE GREEN AND THE RED SOCIETIES... SO MANY OTHERS. MOST RECENTLY WE HAVE BEEN CALLED THE THULE SOCIETY.

"WE"? IF YOU'RE NOT A NAZI, THEN WHAT ARE YOU?

"WE ARE ALL OF THOSE. AND NONE.

"WE HAVE A THOUSAND TENTACLES COILED INTO EVERY ASPECT OF HISTORY, POLITICS, SCIENCE, MAGIC AND FAITH.

"HITLER IS BUT ONE TENTACLE. TOJO AND MUSSOLINI AS WELL. NAPOLEON, THE MEDICIS, TORQUEMADA...THERE HAVE BEEN SO MANY.

"MANY HAVE FALLEN BUT WE-- THE *TRUE MASTERS OF DARKNESS* ON THIS PLANET-- ALWAYS SURVIVE. HITLER WILL FALL. WHO CARES?

"CUT OFF ONE TENTACLE, ONE ARM...

"...AND TWO MORE WILL TAKE ITS PLACE."

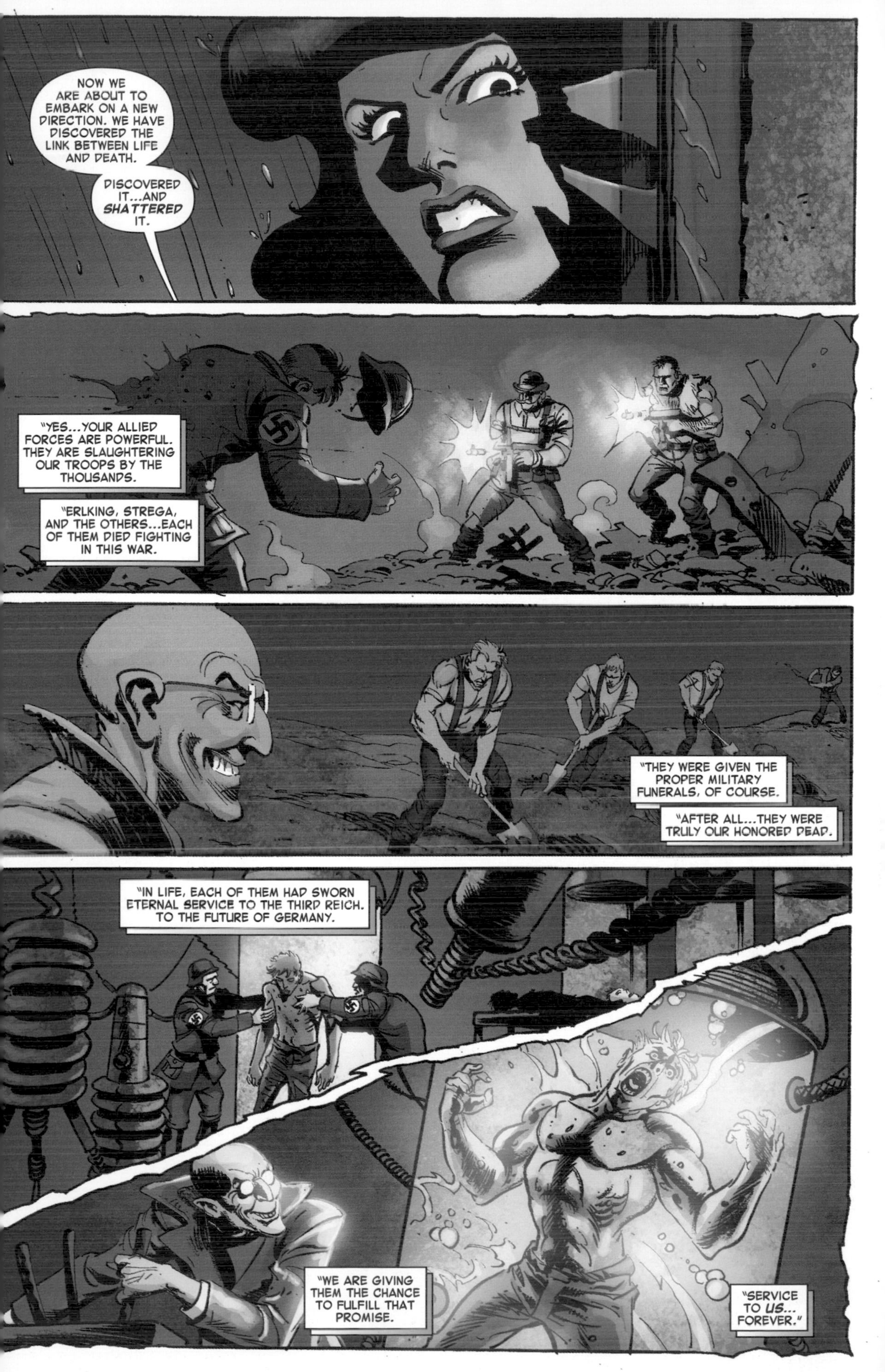
NOW WE ARE ABOUT TO EMBARK ON A NEW DIRECTION. WE HAVE DISCOVERED THE LINK BETWEEN LIFE AND DEATH.
DISCOVERED IT...AND SHATTERED IT.
"YES...YOUR ALLIED FORCES ARE POWERFUL. THEY ARE SLAUGHTERING OUR TROOPS BY THE THOUSANDS.
"ERLKING, STREGA, AND THE OTHERS...EACH OF THEM DIED FIGHTING IN THIS WAR.
"THEY WERE GIVEN THE PROPER MILITARY FUNERALS, OF COURSE.
"AFTER ALL...THEY WERE TRULY OUR HONORED DEAD.
"IN LIFE, EACH OF THEM HAD SWORN ETERNAL SERVICE TO THE THIRD REICH. TO THE FUTURE OF GERMANY.
"WE ARE GIVING THEM THE CHANCE TO FULFILL THAT PROMISE.
"SERVICE TO US... FOREVER."

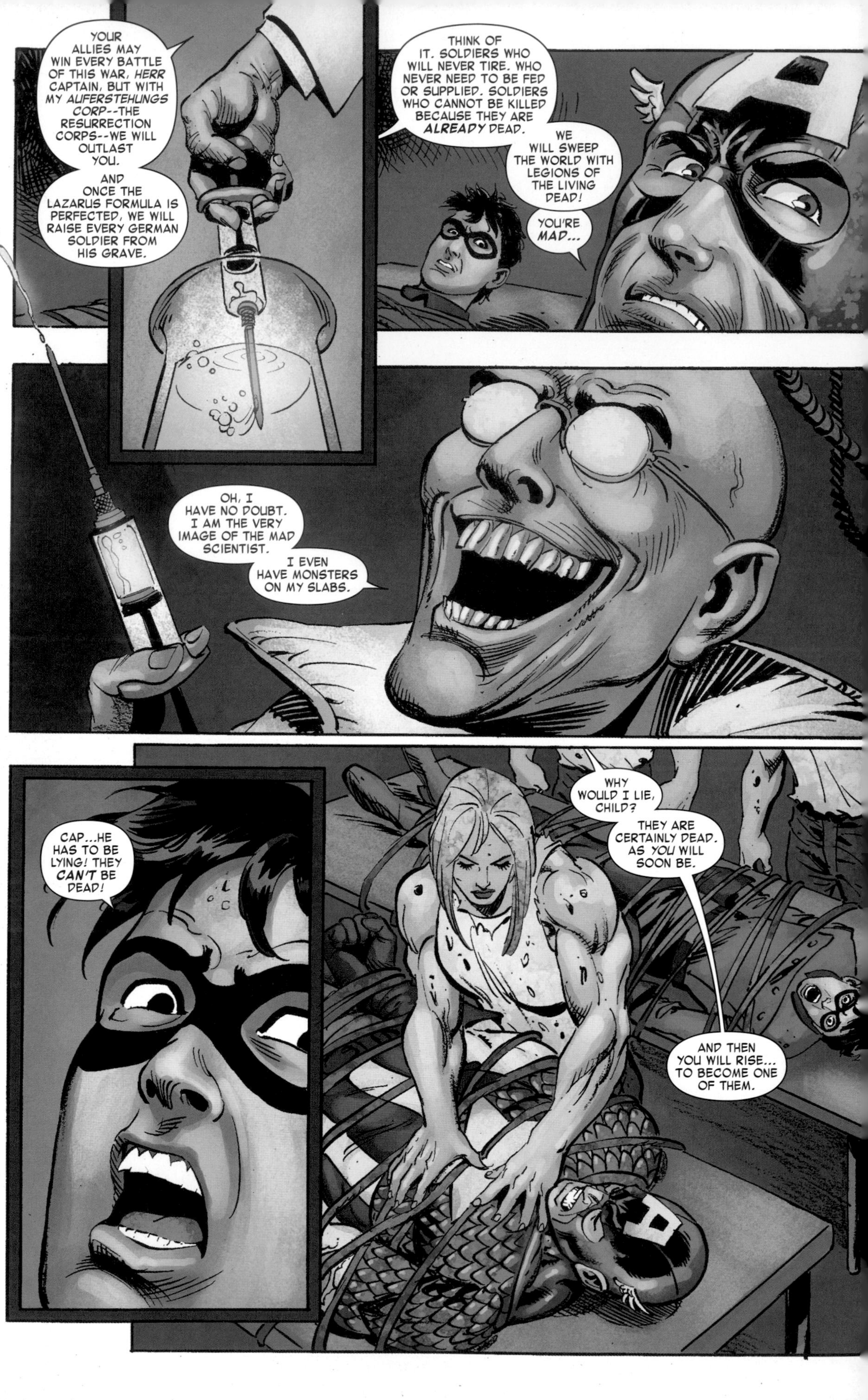
YOUR ALLIES MAY WIN EVERY BATTLE OF THIS WAR, *HERR* CAPTAIN, BUT WITH MY *AUFERSTEHUNGS CORP*--THE RESURRECTION CORPS--WE WILL OUTLAST YOU.
AND ONCE THE LAZARUS FORMULA IS PERFECTED, WE WILL RAISE EVERY GERMAN SOLDIER FROM HIS GRAVE.
THINK OF IT. SOLDIERS WHO WILL NEVER TIRE. WHO NEVER NEED TO BE FED OR SUPPLIED. SOLDIERS WHO CANNOT BE KILLED BECAUSE THEY ARE ***ALREADY*** DEAD.
WE WILL SWEEP THE WORLD WITH LEGIONS OF THE LIVING DEAD!
YOU'RE ***MAD...***
OH, I HAVE NO DOUBT. I AM THE VERY IMAGE OF THE MAD SCIENTIST.
I EVEN HAVE MONSTERS ON MY SLABS.
CAP...HE HAS TO BE LYING! THEY ***CAN'T*** BE DEAD!
WHY WOULD I LIE, CHILD?
THEY ARE CERTAINLY DEAD. AS *YOU* WILL SOON BE.
AND THEN YOU WILL RISE... TO BECOME ONE OF THEM.

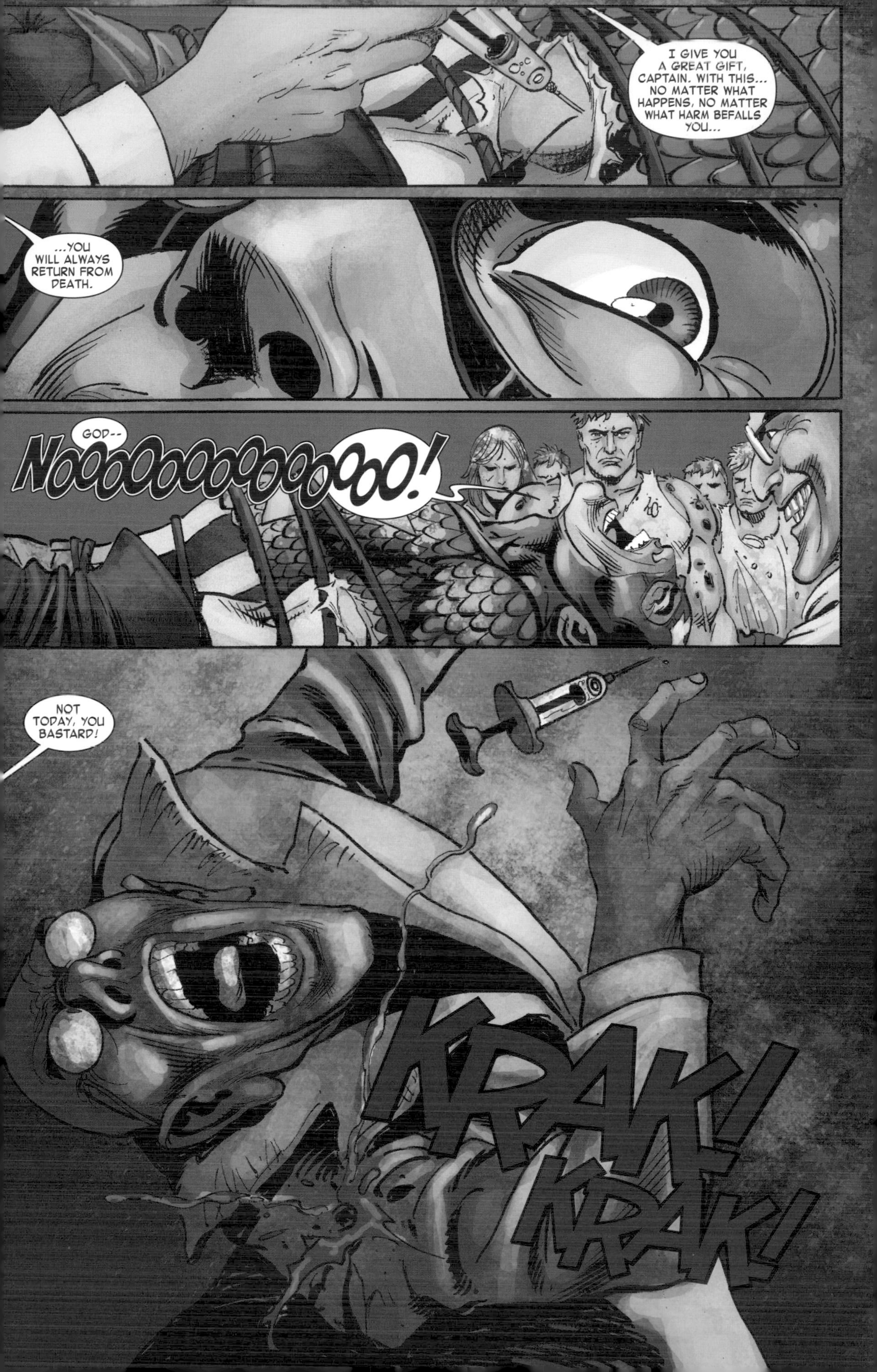
I GIVE YOU A GREAT GIFT, CAPTAIN. WITH THIS... NO MATTER WHAT HAPPENS, NO MATTER WHAT HARM BEFALLS YOU...
...YOU WILL ALWAYS RETURN FROM DEATH.
GOD--
NOOOOOOOOOOOOOO!
NOT TODAY, YOU BASTARD!
KRAK!
KRAK!

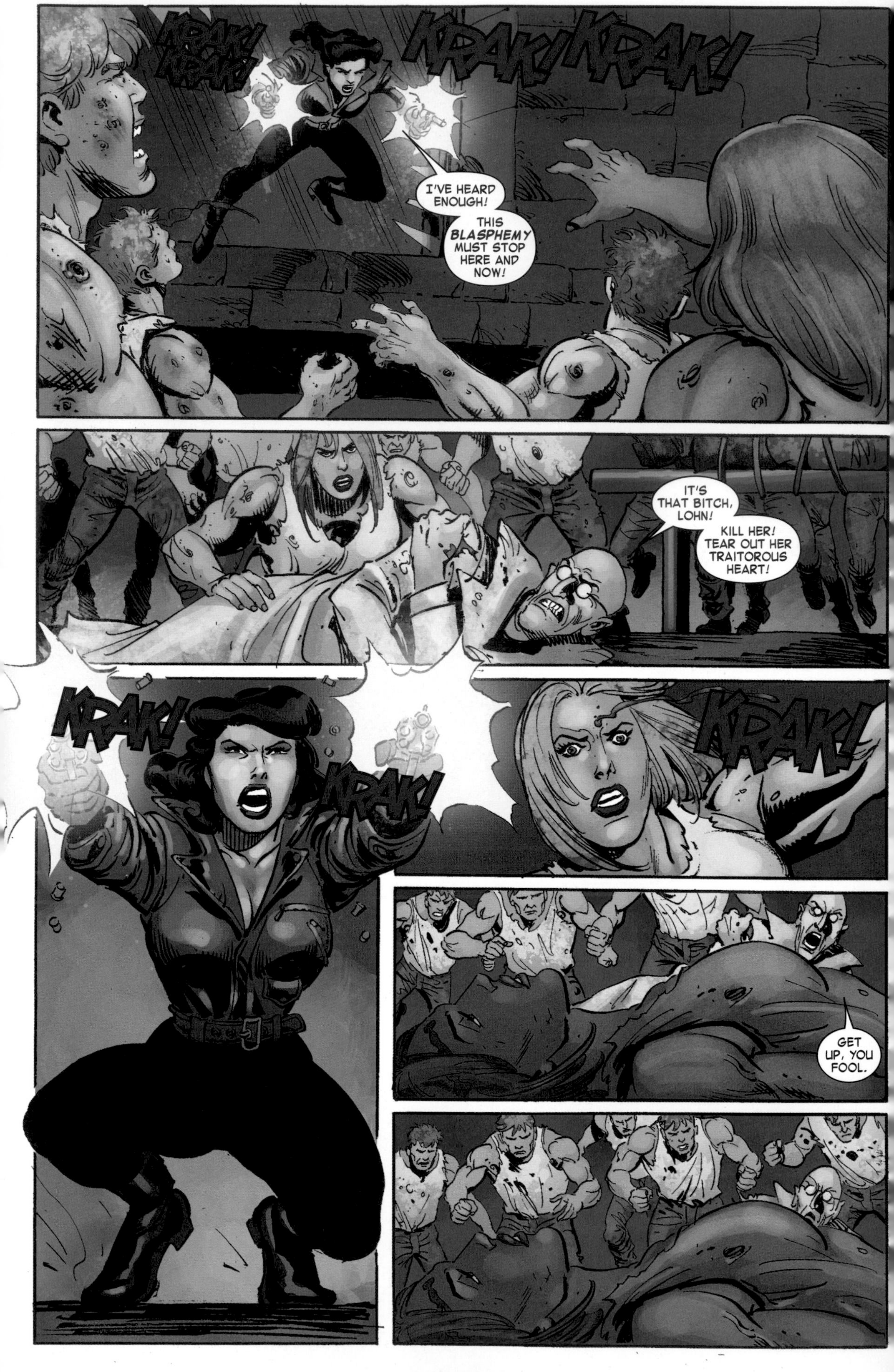
KRAK! KRAK!
KRAK! KRAK!
I'VE HEARD ENOUGH!
THIS BLASPHEMY MUST STOP HERE AND NOW!
IT'S THAT BITCH, LOHN!
KILL HER! TEAR OUT HER TRAITOROUS HEART!
KRAK!
KRAK!
KRAK!
GET UP, YOU FOOL.

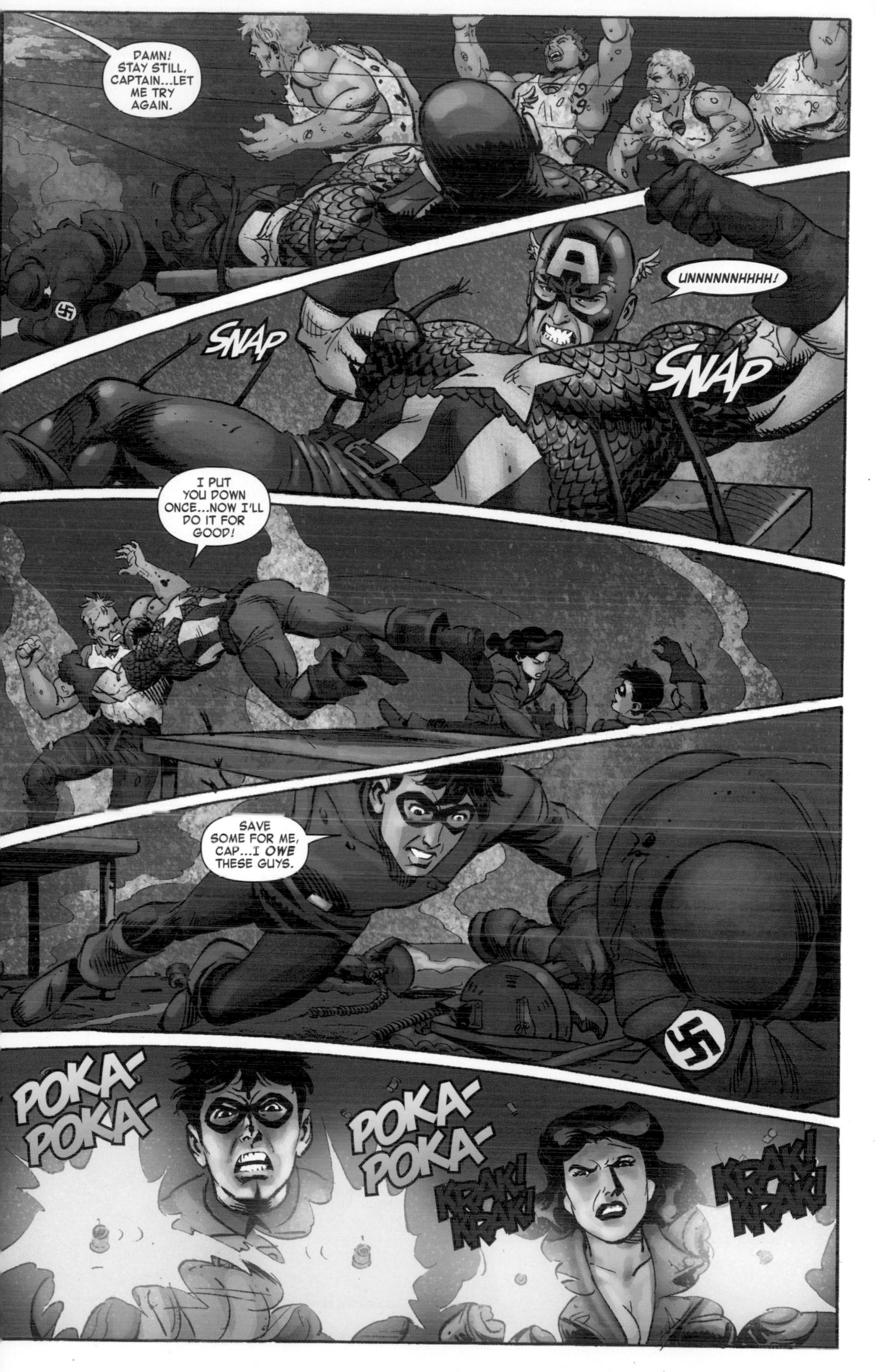
DAMN! STAY STILL, CAPTAIN...LET ME TRY AGAIN.
UNNNNNNHHHH!
SNAP
SNAP
I PUT YOU DOWN ONCE...NOW I'LL DO IT FOR GOOD!
SAVE SOME FOR ME, CAP...I OWE THESE GUYS.
POKA-POKA-
POKA-POKA-
KRAK! KRAK!
KRAK! KRAK!

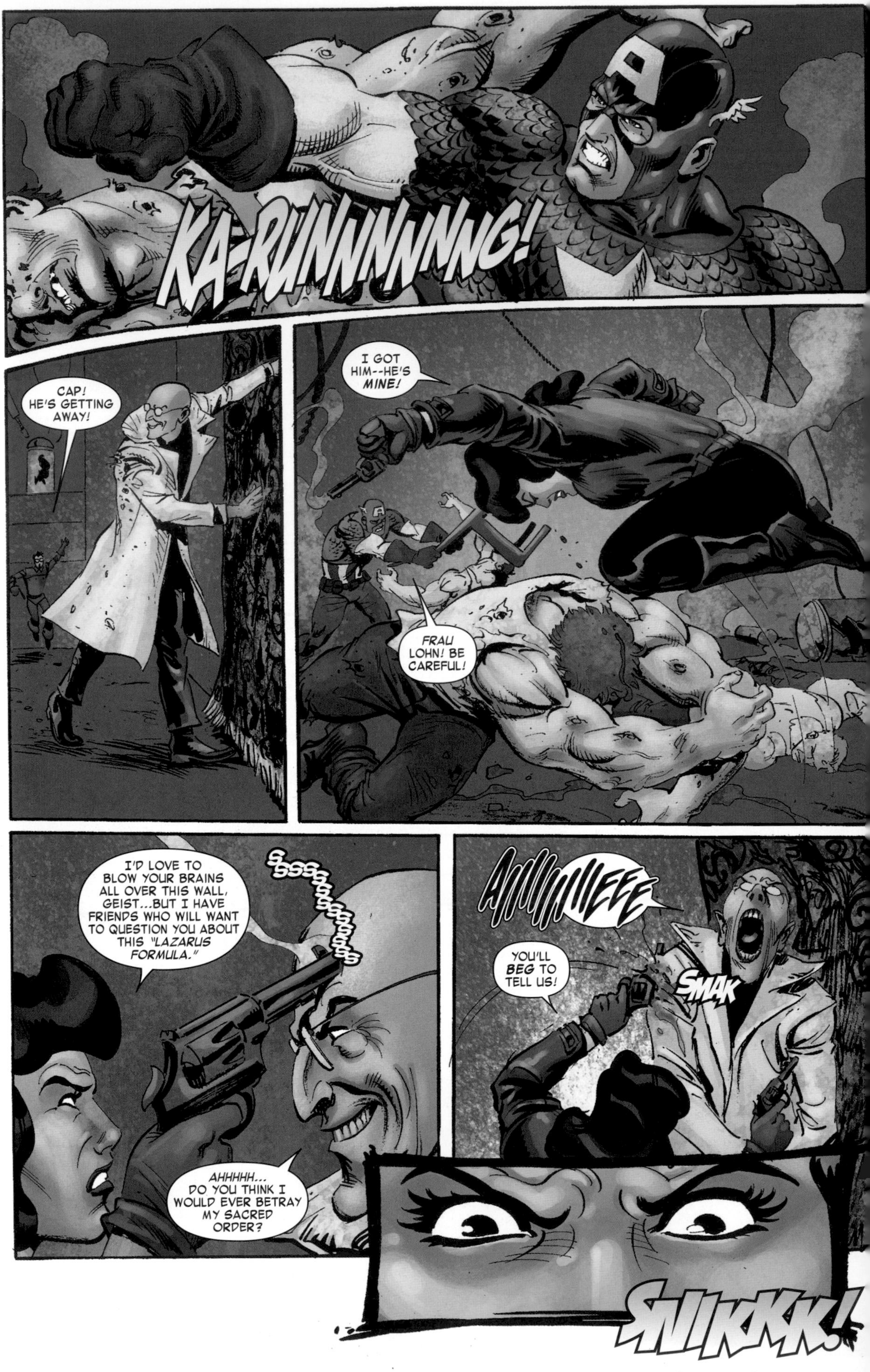
KA-RUNNNNNNG!
CAP! HE'S GETTING AWAY!
I GOT HIM--HE'S MINE!
FRAU LOHN! BE CAREFUL!
I'D LOVE TO BLOW YOUR BRAINS ALL OVER THIS WALL, GEIST...BUT I HAVE FRIENDS WHO WILL WANT TO QUESTION YOU ABOUT THIS "LAZARUS FORMULA."
AHHHHH... DO YOU THINK I WOULD EVER BETRAY MY SACRED ORDER?
YOU'LL BEG TO TELL US!
SMAK
SHUKKK!

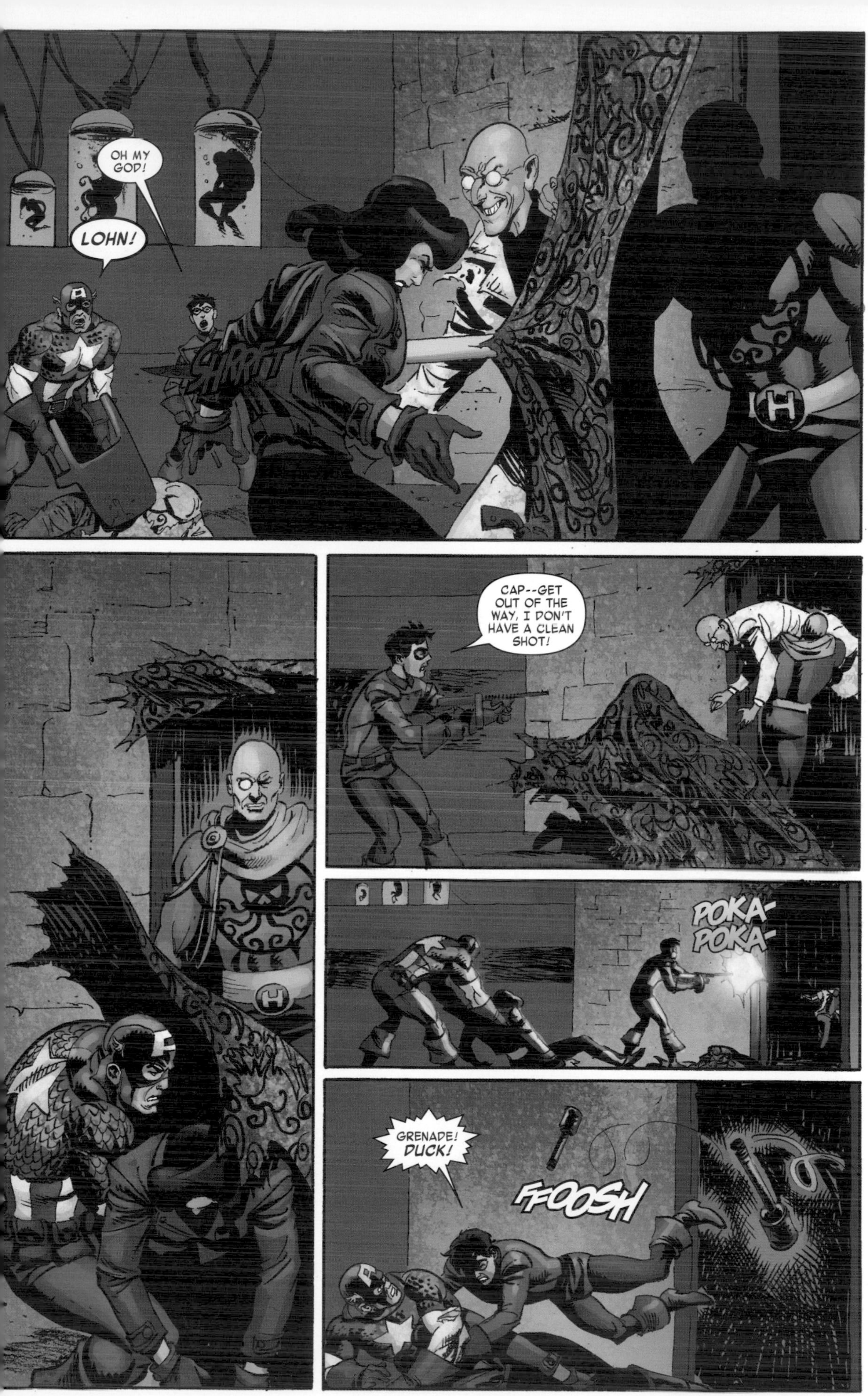
OH MY GOD!
LOHN!
SHRRFT
CAP--GET OUT OF THE WAY, I DON'T HAVE A CLEAN SHOT!
POKA-POKA-
GRENADE! DUCK!
FFOOSH

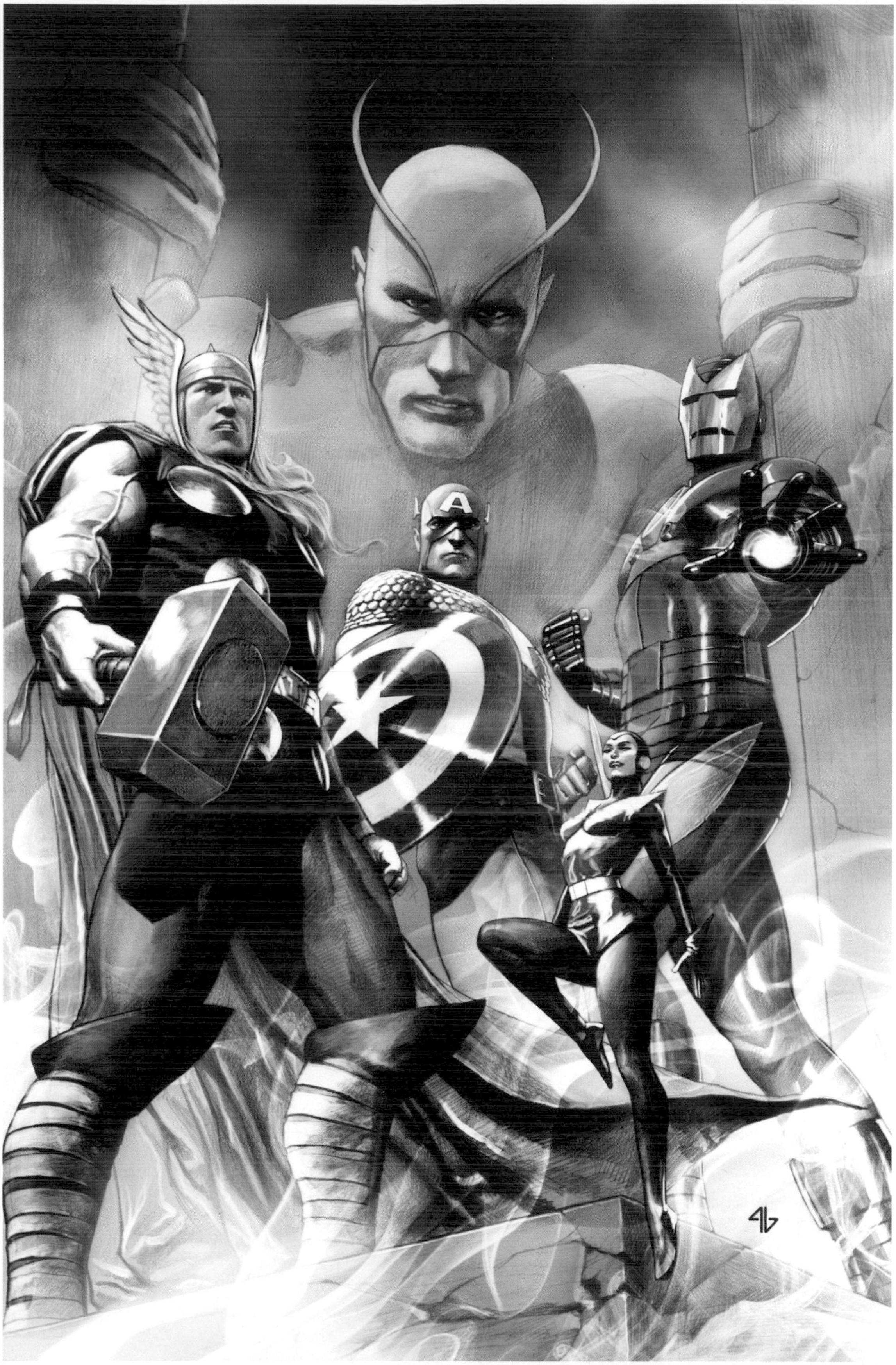

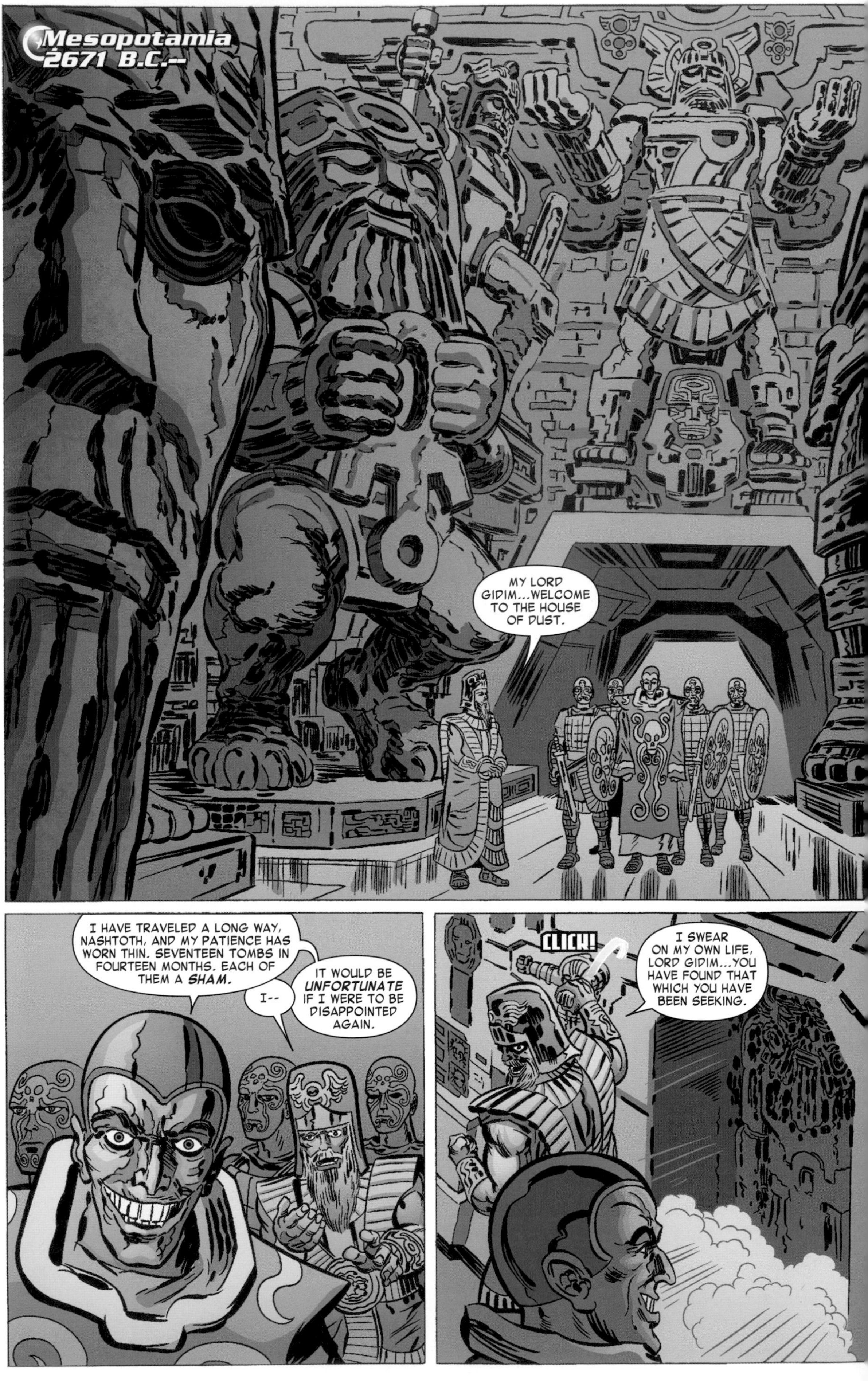
Mesopotamia 2671 B.C.--
MY LORD GIDIM...WELCOME TO THE HOUSE OF DUST.
I HAVE TRAVELED A LONG WAY, NASHTOTH, AND MY PATIENCE HAS WORN THIN. SEVENTEEN TOMBS IN FOURTEEN MONTHS. EACH OF THEM A SHAM.
I--
IT WOULD BE UNFORTUNATE IF I WERE TO BE DISAPPOINTED AGAIN.
CLICK!
I SWEAR ON MY OWN LIFE, LORD GIDIM...YOU HAVE FOUND THAT WHICH YOU HAVE BEEN SEEKING.

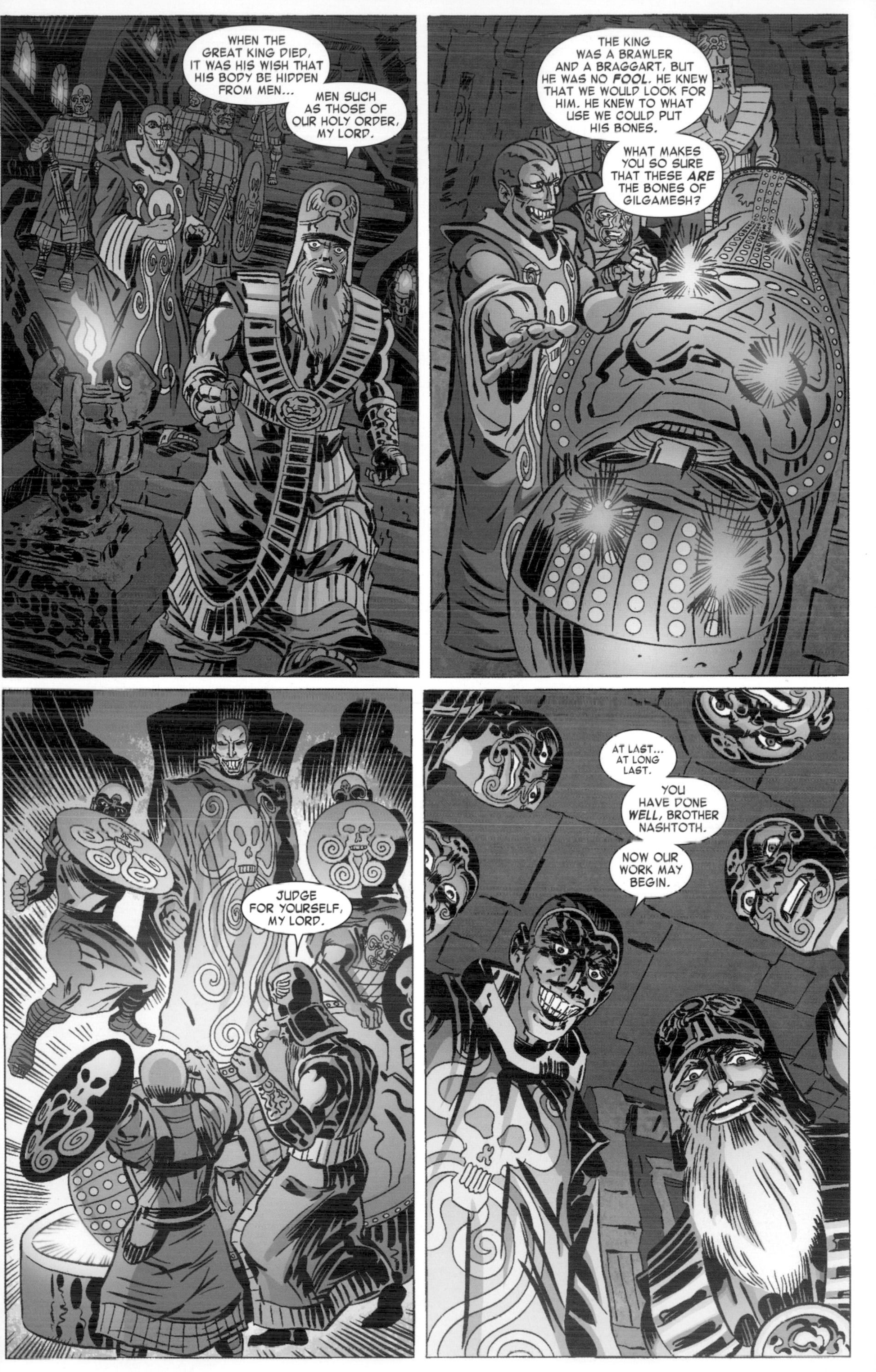

WHEN THE GREAT KING DIED, IT WAS HIS WISH THAT HIS BODY BE HIDDEN FROM MEN...
MEN SUCH AS THOSE OF OUR HOLY ORDER, MY LORD.
THE KING WAS A BRAWLER AND A BRAGGART, BUT HE WAS NO FOOL. HE KNEW THAT WE WOULD LOOK FOR HIM. HE KNEW TO WHAT USE WE COULD PUT HIS BONES.
WHAT MAKES YOU SO SURE THAT THESE ARE THE BONES OF GILGAMESH?
JUDGE FOR YOURSELF, MY LORD.
AT LAST... AT LONG LAST.
YOU HAVE DONE WELL, BROTHER NASHTOTH.
NOW OUR WORK MAY BEGIN.

IT'S WONDERFUL TO SEE YOU. BUT WHY HERE...AND WHY NOW?

I DON'T KNOW HOW MUCH HISTORY YOU'VE CAUGHT UP WITH SINCE YOUR "RETURN," BUT FOR SOME OF US THE WAR NEVER ENDED. WE TRADED ONE EVIL FOR ANOTHER.

AFTER HITLER FELL, GERMANY WAS TORN APART. YOU SLEPT THROUGH THE COLD WAR...BUT MY RESISTANCE CELL NEVER STOPPED FIGHTING.

WHEN THE WALL FELL, GREATER EVILS ROSE. THE BAADER-MEINHOF GANG AND THEIR RED ARMY FACTION, THE GERMAN PEOPLE'S UNION, DER REPUBLIKANERS, NEO-NAZIS. MANY FACES OF THE SAME MONSTER.

LIKE THE NAZIS BEFORE THEM, THESE NEW ORGANIZATIONS OFTEN LOOKED TO SCIENCE TO PROVIDE THEM WITH WEAPONS OF CONQUEST AND TERROR.

MY GROUP INFILTRATES THESE ORGANIZATIONS. WE LOCATE THE SCIENTISTS-- MANY OF WHOM ARE WORKING UNDER DURESS...

AND YOU RESCUE THEM?

WHEN WE CAN.

THIS IS WAR, CAPTAIN. THERE ARE ALWAYS SACRIFICES.

RECENTLY I WAS ABLE TO SMUGGLE OUT A KEY SCIENTIST. DR. HOMLER. HE WAS WORKING ON A SPECIAL PROJECT THAT HAS TIES TO PROJEKT AUFERSTEHUNGS.

THAT WAS DR. GEIST'S PROJECT. THE RESURRECTION CORPS AND THE LAZARUS PATHOGEN. WE TORE THAT DOWN...DESTROYED THE WHOLE LAB.

OF COURSE WE DIDN'T DESTROY IT. I FIGURED YOU KNEW THAT. I BROUGHT THE COMPLETE DOSSIER AS YOU REQUESTED IN YOUR NOTE.

MY NOTE? BUT...YOU ASKED ME TO MEET...

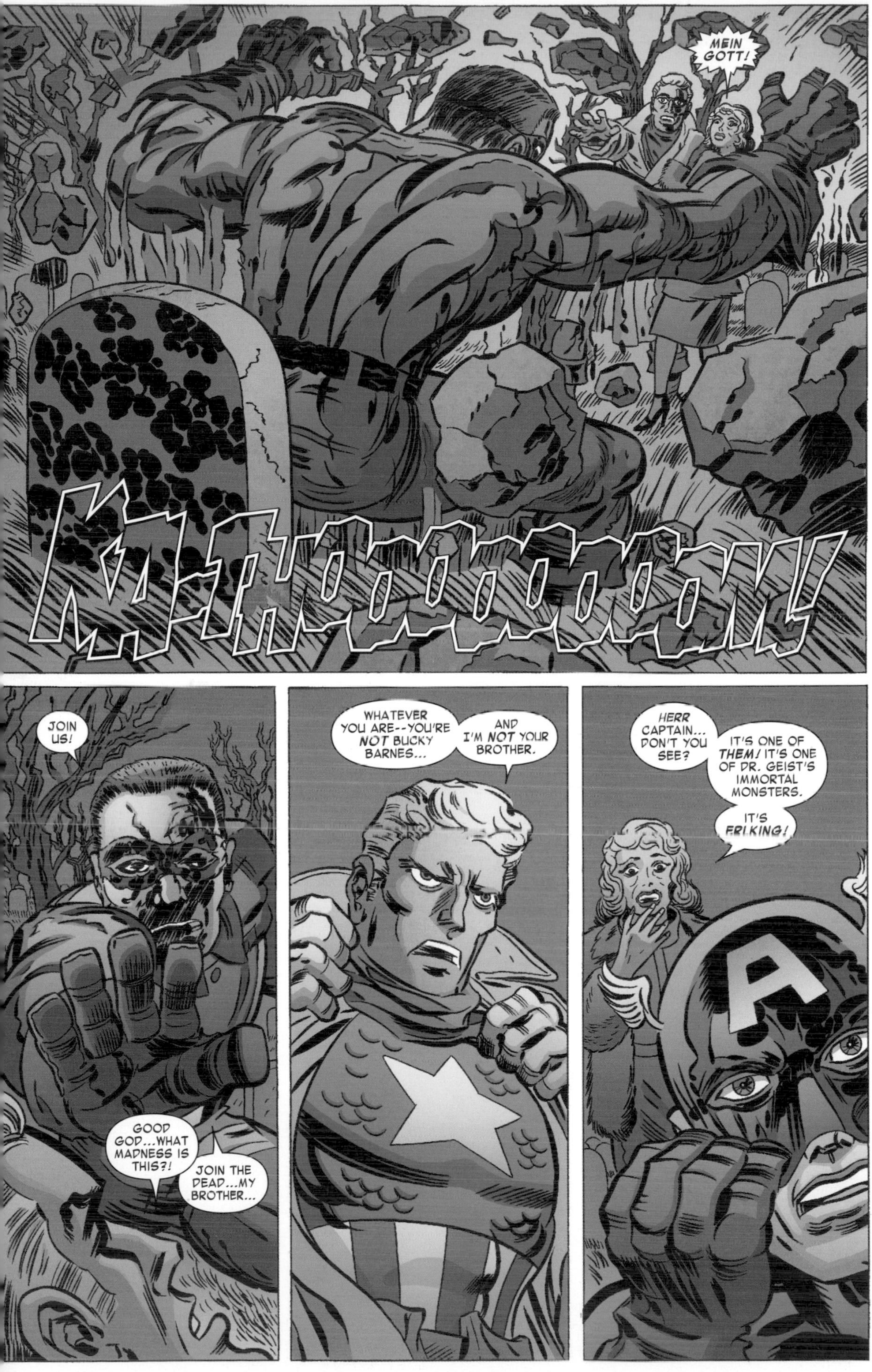
MEIN GOTT!
KA-THOOOOOOOOM!
JOIN US!
GOOD GOD...WHAT MADNESS IS THIS?!
JOIN THE DEAD...MY BROTHER...
WHATEVER YOU ARE--YOU'RE NOT BUCKY BARNES...
AND I'M NOT YOUR BROTHER.
HERR CAPTAIN... DON'T YOU SEE?
IT'S ONE OF THEM! IT'S ONE OF DR. GEIST'S IMMORTAL MONSTERS.
IT'S ERLKING!

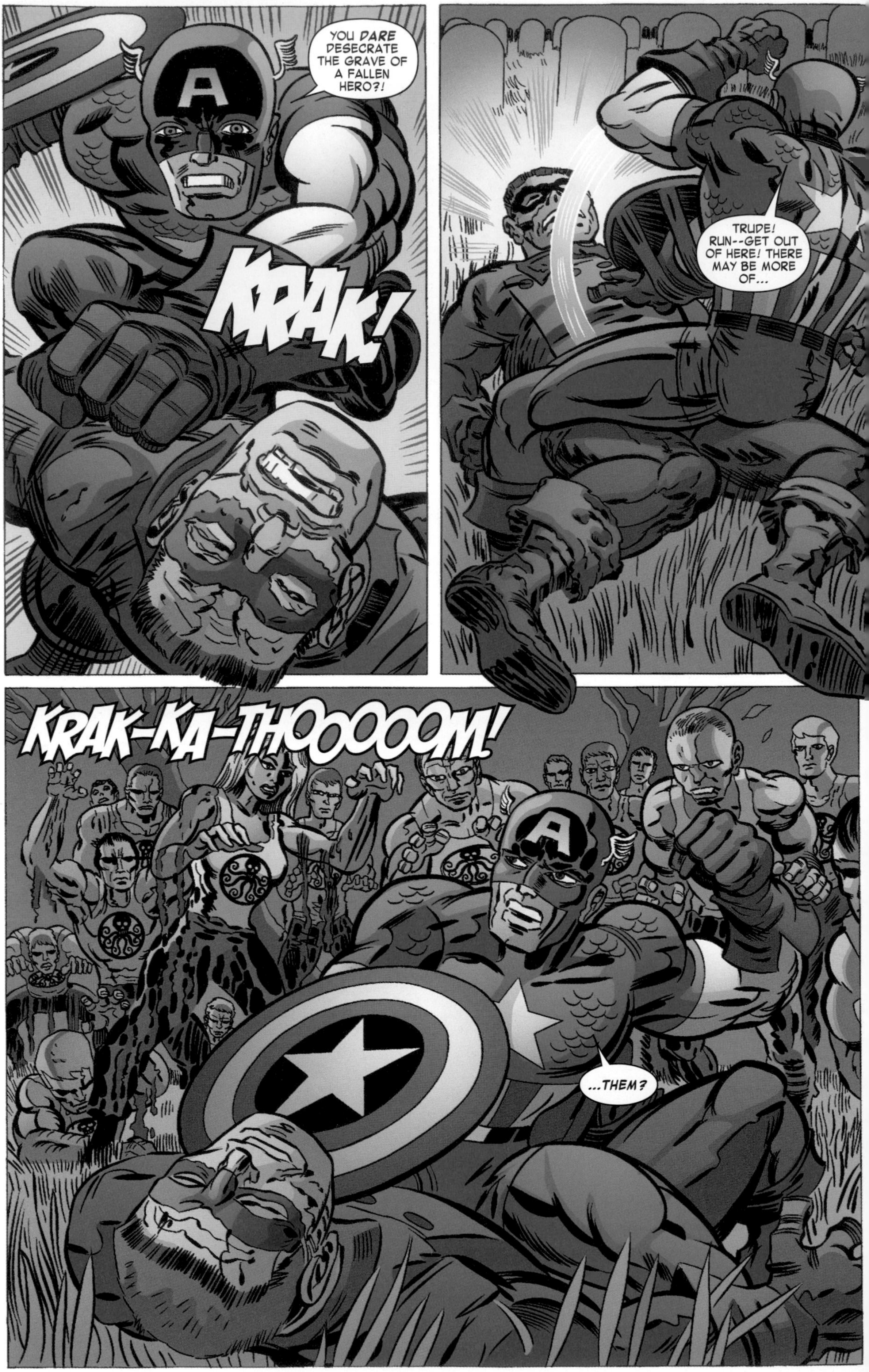
YOU DARE DESECRATE THE GRAVE OF A FALLEN HERO?!
KRAK!
TRUDE! RUN--GET OUT OF HERE! THERE MAY BE MORE OF...
KRAK-KA-THOOOOOM!
...THEM?

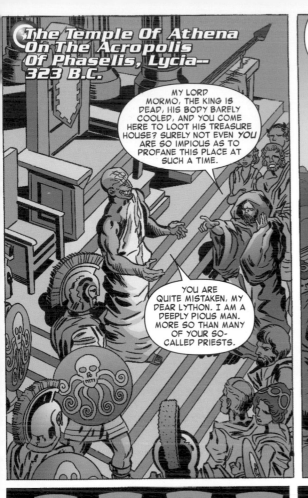

MY LORD MORMO, THE KING IS DEAD, HIS BODY BARELY COOLED, AND YOU COME HERE TO LOOT HIS TREASURE HOUSE? SURELY NOT EVEN *YOU* ARE SO IMPIOUS AS TO PROFANE THIS PLACE AT SUCH A TIME.

YOU ARE QUITE MISTAKEN, MY DEAR LYTHON. I AM A DEEPLY PIOUS MAN. MORE SO THAN MANY OF YOUR SO-CALLED PRIESTS.

I WAS *WITH* ALEXANDER WHEN HE PAID HALF HIS TREASURY TO PURCHASE THE HOLY SPEAR. I KNOW WHAT THE SPEAR OF ACHILLES MEANT TO HIM. IT WAS HIS BY RIGHT.

ALEXANDER, SON OF OLYMPIAS, WAS DESCENDED THROUGH ANTIQUITY FROM NEOPTOLEMUS, SON OF ACHILLES.

ACHILLES, SON OF THE NYMPH THETIS... FEARED BY ZEUS HIMSELF.

ACHILLES' BLOOD IS CRUSTED INTO THE BLADE. THE BLOOD OF AN IMMORTAL. AND THE KEY TO IMMORTALITY...

I KNOW FULL WELL OF YOUR DARK SCHEMES--YOU AND THE TWISTED SORCERERS OF THE ORDER OF THE *HYDRA.* YOU DARE NOT PROFANE THIS HOLY RELIC WITH YOUR--

YOU WOULD FIND THAT THE WORK WE DO IS THE HOLIEST PURPOSE OF ALL.

IF YOU WERE ALIVE TO SEE IT. AH WELL.

URK!

CHUNK

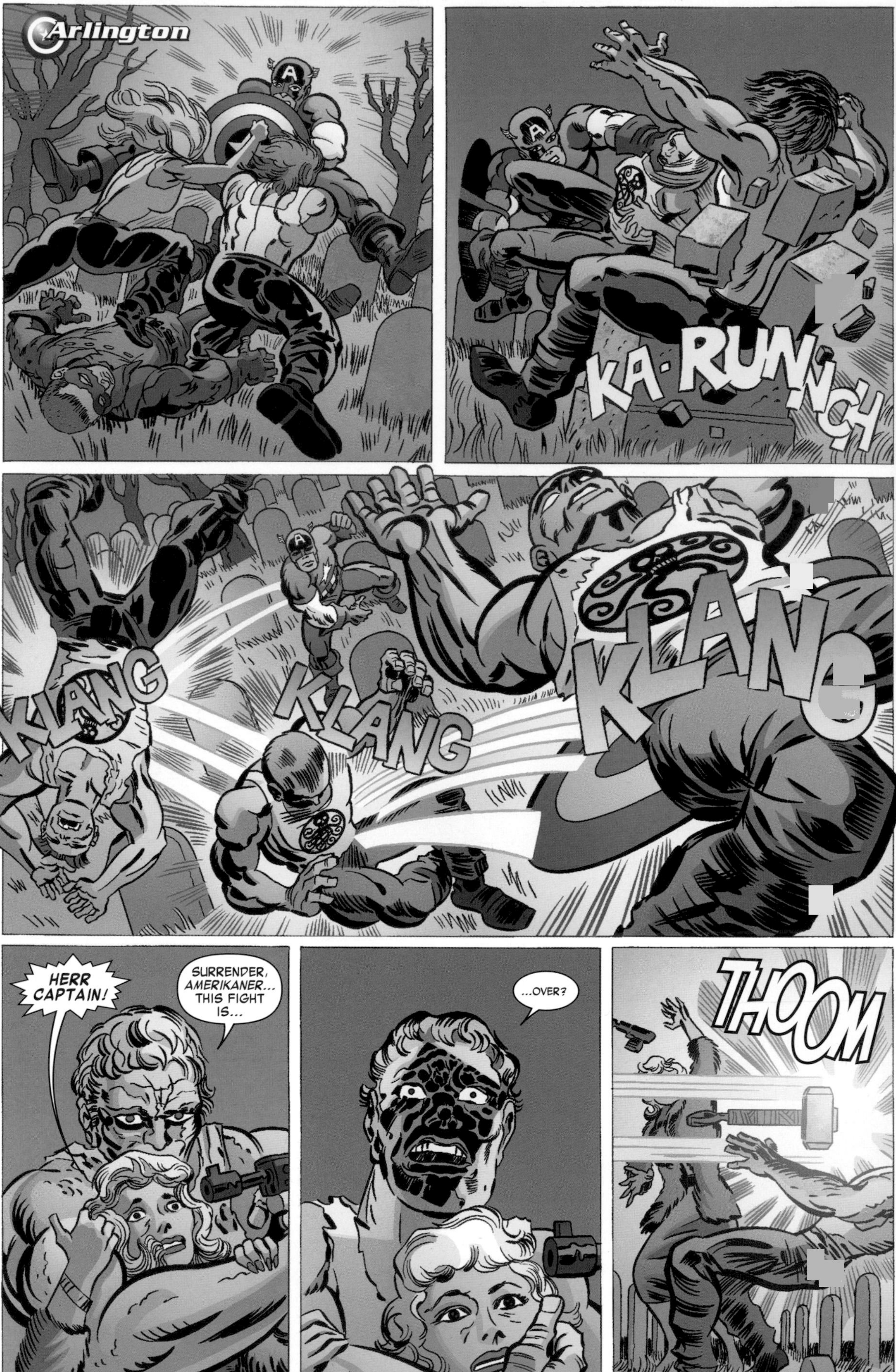
Arlington
KA-RUNNCH
KLANG
KLANG
KLANG
HERR CAPTAIN!
SURRENDER, AMERIKANER... THIS FIGHT IS...
...OVER?
THOOM

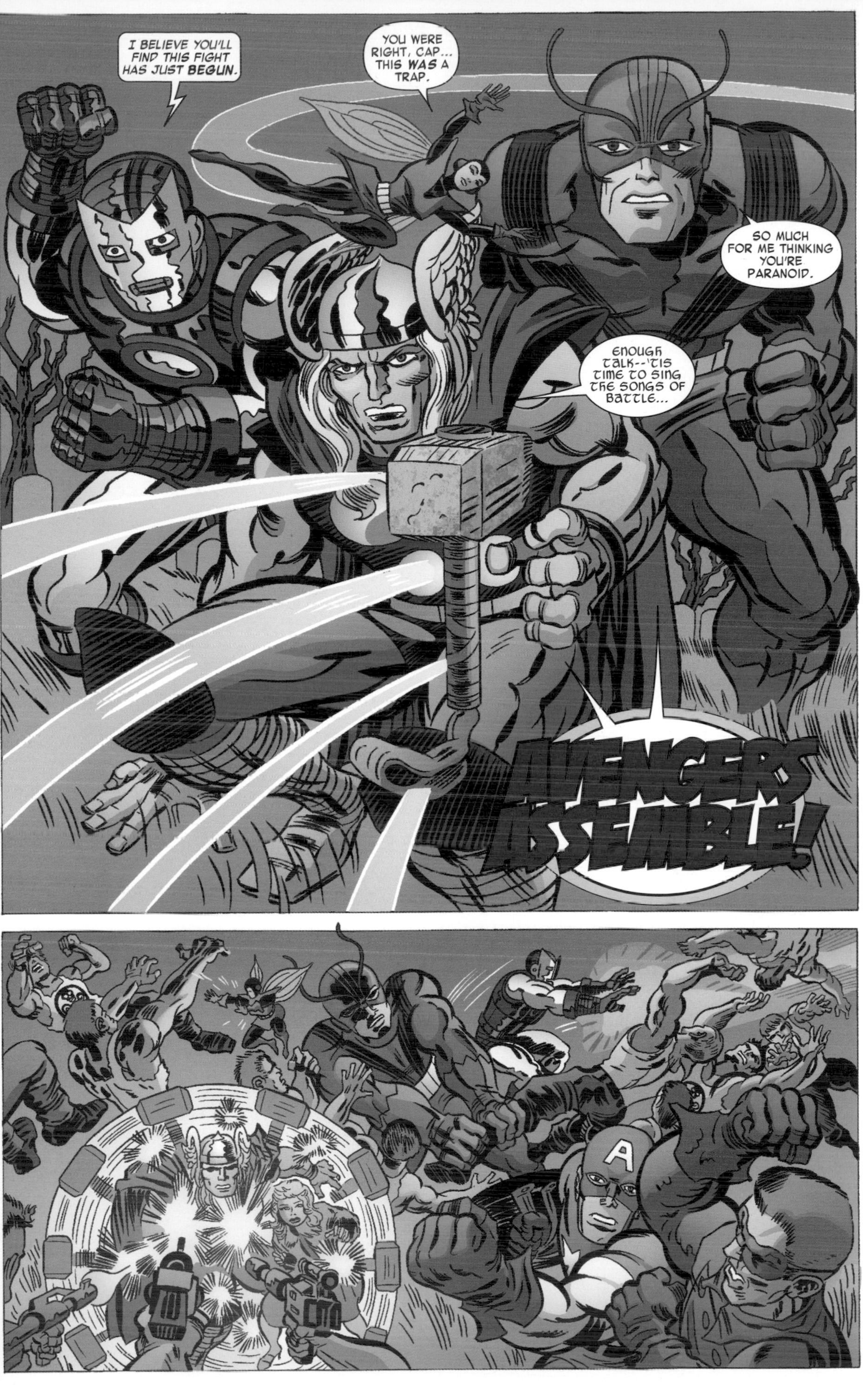
I BELIEVE YOU'LL FIND THIS FIGHT HAS JUST BEGUN.
YOU WERE RIGHT, CAP... THIS WAS A TRAP.
SO MUCH FOR ME THINKING YOU'RE PARANOID.
ENOUGH TALK--'TIS TIME TO SING THE SONGS OF BATTLE...
AVENGERS ASSEMBLE!

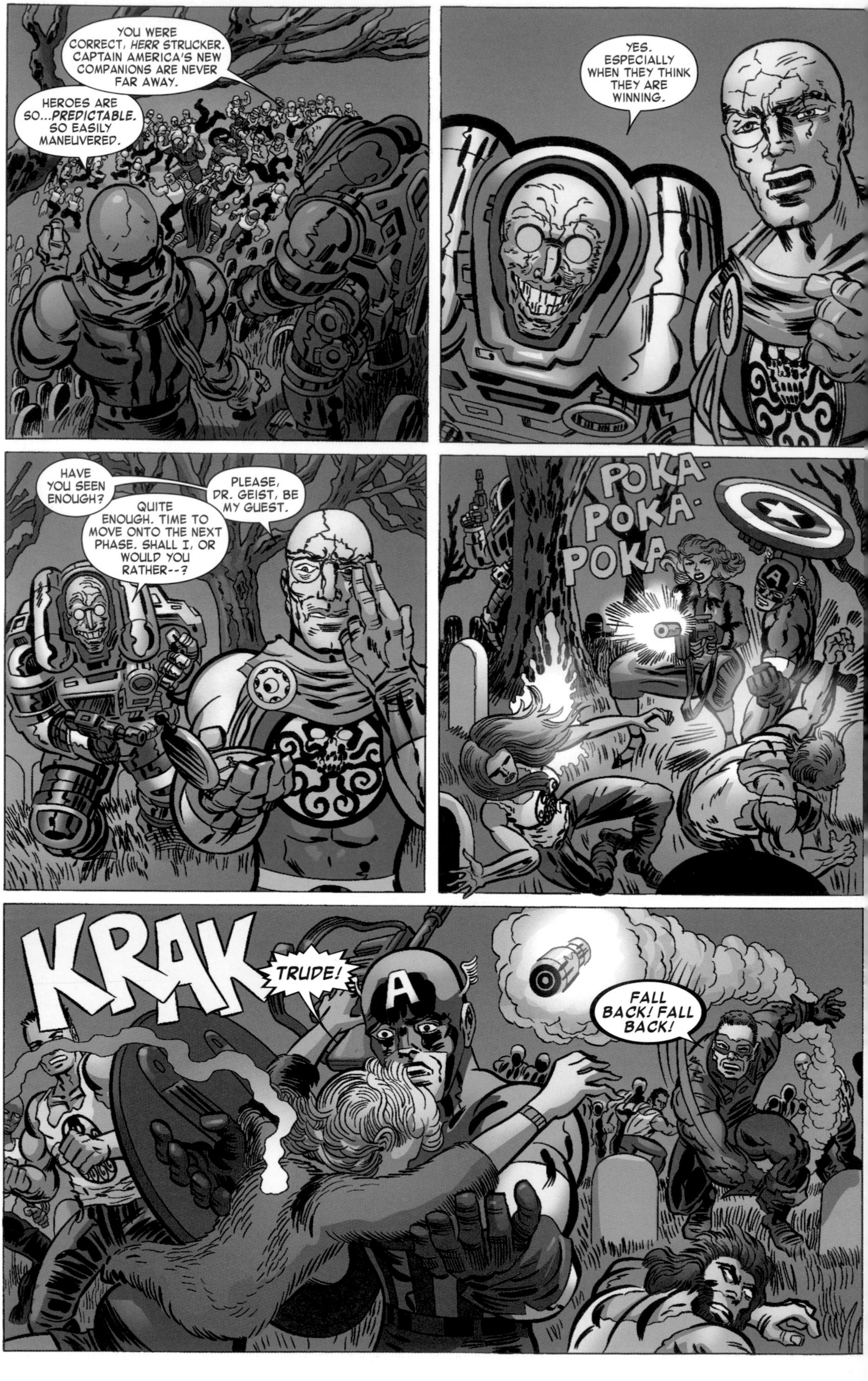
YOU WERE CORRECT, *HERR* STRUCKER. CAPTAIN AMERICA'S NEW COMPANIONS ARE NEVER FAR AWAY.
HEROES ARE SO...*PREDICTABLE.* SO EASILY MANEUVERED.
YES. ESPECIALLY WHEN THEY THINK THEY ARE WINNING.
HAVE YOU SEEN ENOUGH?
QUITE ENOUGH. TIME TO MOVE ONTO THE NEXT PHASE. SHALL I, OR WOULD YOU RATHER--?
PLEASE, DR. GEIST, BE MY GUEST.
POKA-
POKA-
POKA
KRAK
TRUDE!
FALL BACK! FALL BACK!

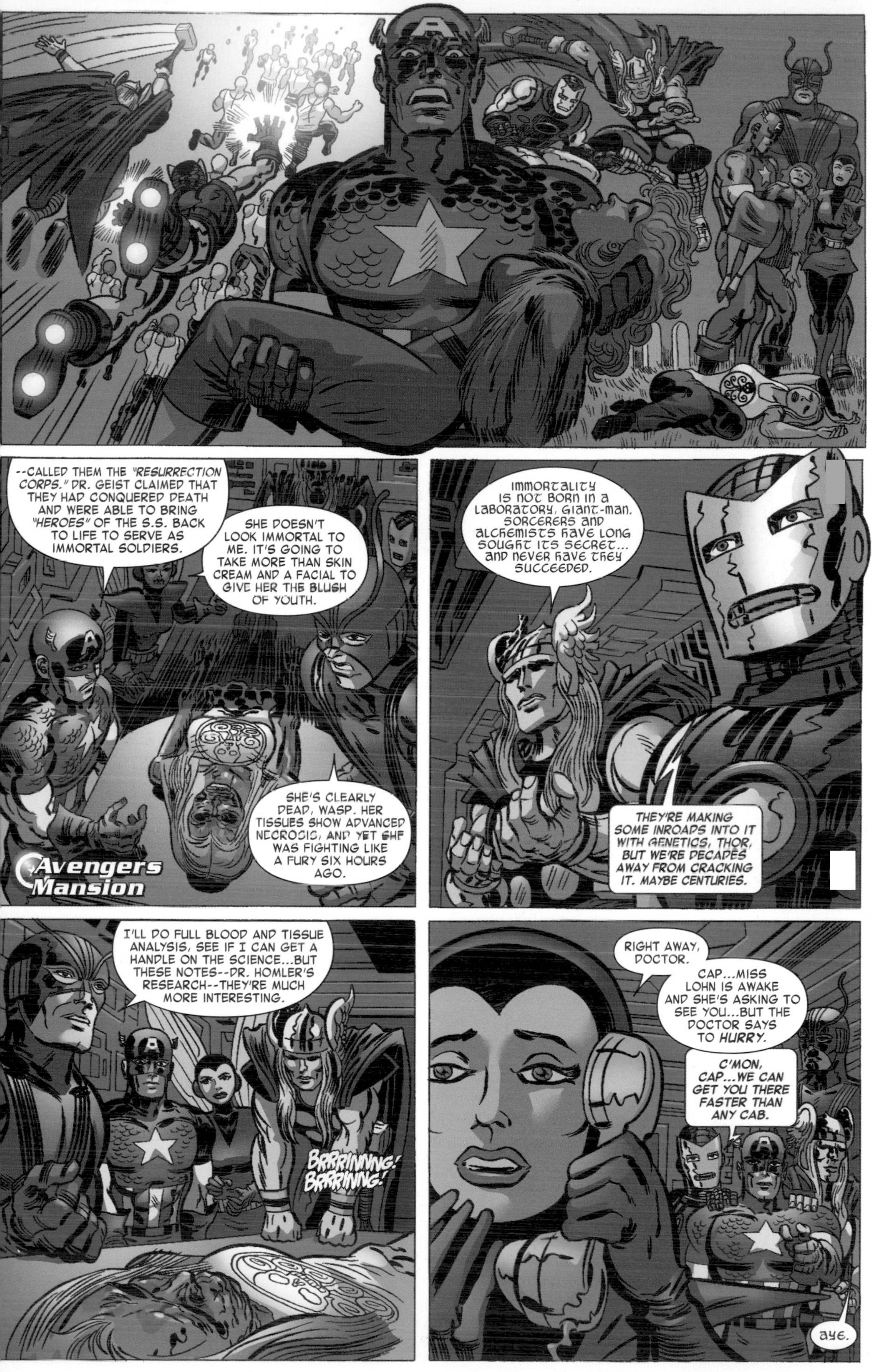

--CALLED THEM THE "RESURRECTION CORPS." DR. GEIST CLAIMED THAT THEY HAD CONQUERED DEATH AND WERE ABLE TO BRING "HEROES" OF THE S.S. BACK TO LIFE TO SERVE AS IMMORTAL SOLDIERS.
SHE DOESN'T LOOK IMMORTAL TO ME. IT'S GOING TO TAKE MORE THAN SKIN CREAM AND A FACIAL TO GIVE HER THE BLUSH OF YOUTH.
SHE'S CLEARLY DEAD, WASP. HER TISSUES SHOW ADVANCED NECROSIS, AND YET SHE WAS FIGHTING LIKE A FURY SIX HOURS AGO.
Avengers Mansion
IMMORTALITY IS NOT BORN IN A LABORATORY, GIANT-MAN. SORCERERS AND ALCHEMISTS HAVE LONG SOUGHT ITS SECRET... AND NEVER HAVE THEY SUCCEEDED.
THEY'RE MAKING SOME INROADS INTO IT WITH GENETICS, THOR, BUT WE'RE DECADES AWAY FROM CRACKING IT. MAYBE CENTURIES.
I'LL DO FULL BLOOD AND TISSUE ANALYSIS, SEE IF I CAN GET A HANDLE ON THE SCIENCE...BUT THESE NOTES--DR. HOMLER'S RESEARCH--THEY'RE MUCH MORE INTERESTING.
BRRRINNNG! BRRRINNNG!
RIGHT AWAY, DOCTOR.
CAP...MISS LOHN IS AWAKE AND SHE'S ASKING TO SEE YOU...BUT THE DOCTOR SAYS TO HURRY.
C'MON, CAP...WE CAN GET YOU THERE FASTER THAN ANY CAB.
AYE.

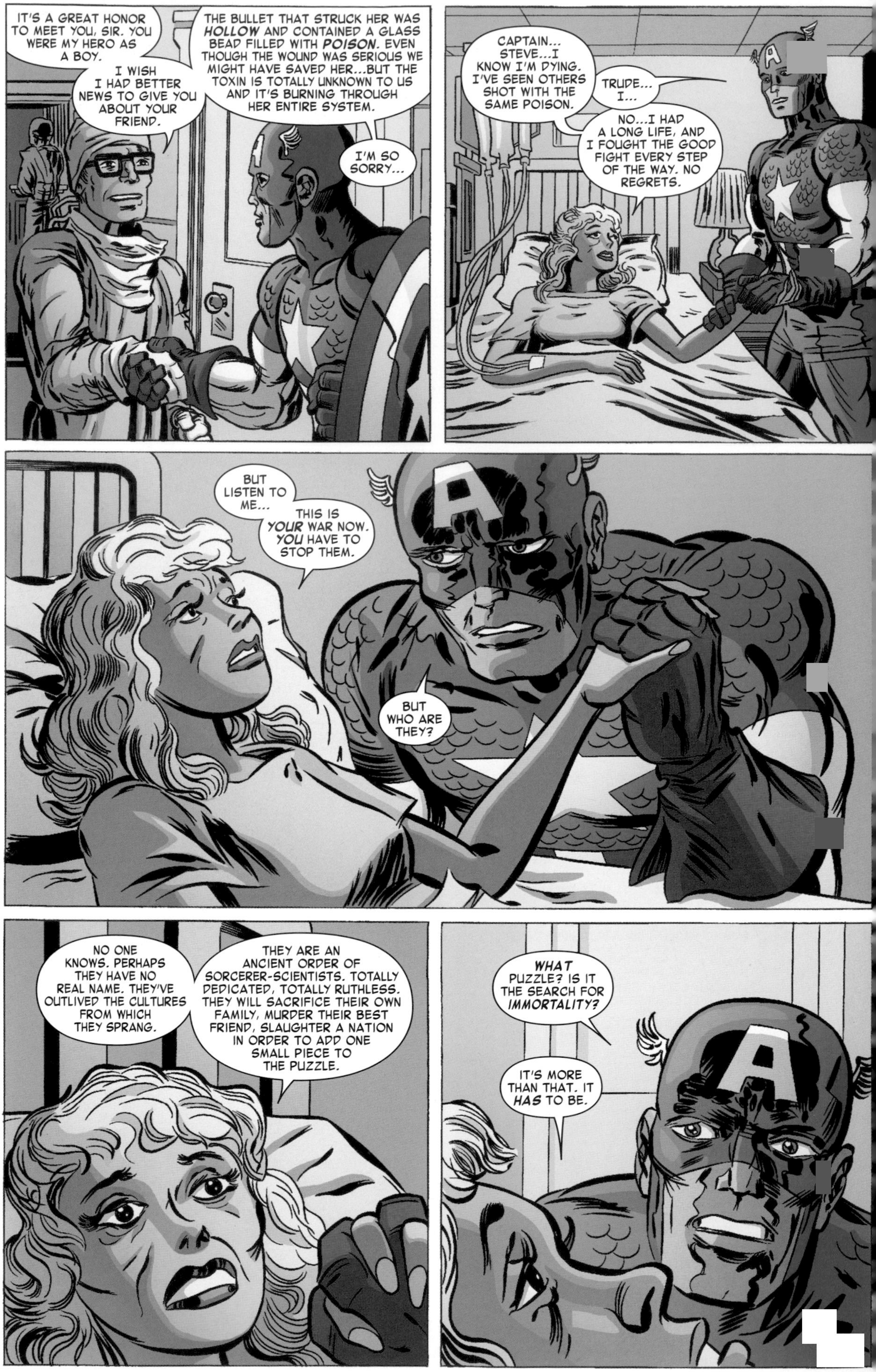

IT'S A GREAT HONOR TO MEET YOU, SIR. YOU WERE MY HERO AS A BOY.
I WISH I HAD BETTER NEWS TO GIVE YOU ABOUT YOUR FRIEND.
THE BULLET THAT STRUCK HER WAS HOLLOW AND CONTAINED A GLASS BEAD FILLED WITH POISON. EVEN THOUGH THE WOUND WAS SERIOUS WE MIGHT HAVE SAVED HER...BUT THE TOXIN IS TOTALLY UNKNOWN TO US AND IT'S BURNING THROUGH HER ENTIRE SYSTEM.
I'M SO SORRY...
CAPTAIN... STEVE...I KNOW I'M DYING. I'VE SEEN OTHERS SHOT WITH THE SAME POISON.
TRUDE... I...
NO...I HAD A LONG LIFE, AND I FOUGHT THE GOOD FIGHT EVERY STEP OF THE WAY. NO REGRETS.
BUT LISTEN TO ME...
THIS IS YOUR WAR NOW. YOU HAVE TO STOP THEM.
BUT WHO ARE THEY?
NO ONE KNOWS. PERHAPS THEY HAVE NO REAL NAME. THEY'VE OUTLIVED THE CULTURES FROM WHICH THEY SPRANG.
THEY ARE AN ANCIENT ORDER OF SORCERER-SCIENTISTS. TOTALLY DEDICATED, TOTALLY RUTHLESS. THEY WILL SACRIFICE THEIR OWN FAMILY, MURDER THEIR BEST FRIEND, SLAUGHTER A NATION IN ORDER TO ADD ONE SMALL PIECE TO THE PUZZLE.
WHAT PUZZLE? IS IT THE SEARCH FOR IMMORTALITY?
IT'S MORE THAN THAT. IT HAS TO BE.

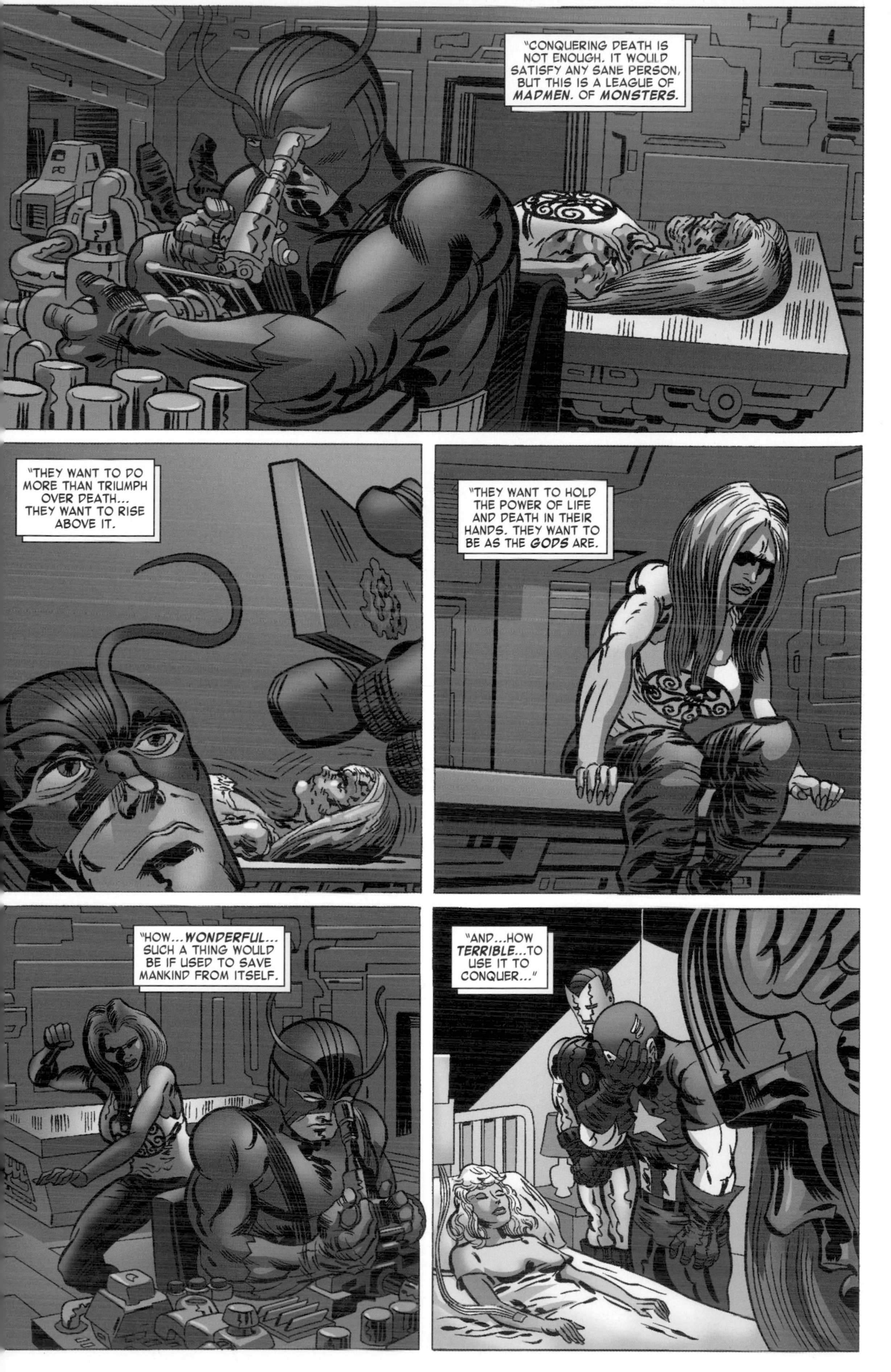
"CONQUERING DEATH IS NOT ENOUGH. IT WOULD SATISFY ANY SANE PERSON, BUT THIS IS A LEAGUE OF *MADMEN*. OF *MONSTERS*.
"THEY WANT TO DO MORE THAN TRIUMPH OVER DEATH... THEY WANT TO RISE ABOVE IT.
"THEY WANT TO HOLD THE POWER OF LIFE AND DEATH IN THEIR HANDS. THEY WANT TO BE AS THE *GODS* ARE.
"HOW...*WONDERFUL*... SUCH A THING WOULD BE IF USED TO SAVE MANKIND FROM ITSELF.
"AND...HOW *TERRIBLE*...TO USE IT TO CONQUER..."

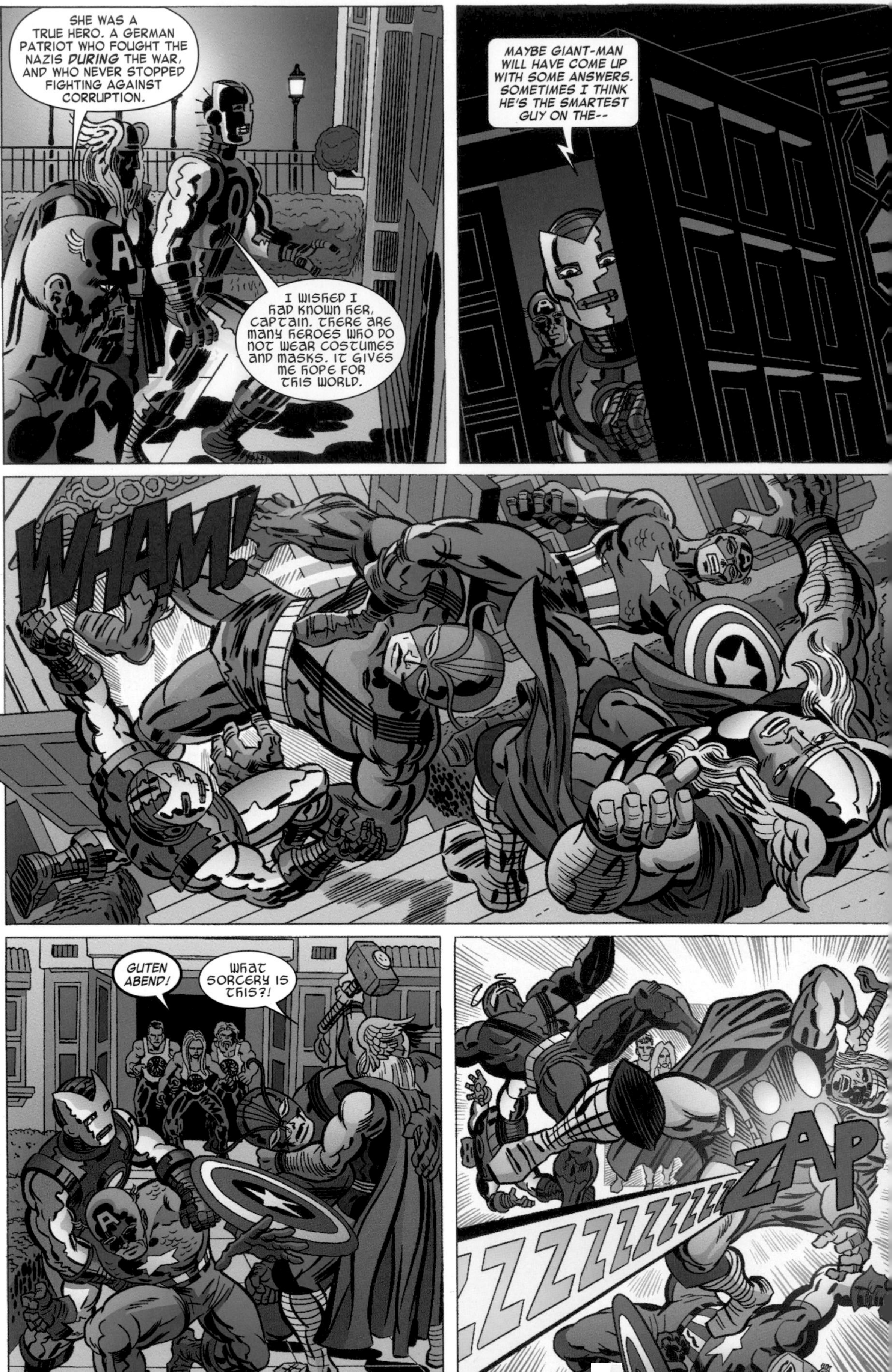
SHE WAS A TRUE HERO. A GERMAN PATRIOT WHO FOUGHT THE NAZIS DURING THE WAR, AND WHO NEVER STOPPED FIGHTING AGAINST CORRUPTION.
I WISHED I HAD KNOWN HER, CAPTAIN. THERE ARE MANY HEROES WHO DO NOT WEAR COSTUMES AND MASKS. IT GIVES ME HOPE FOR THIS WORLD.
MAYBE GIANT-MAN WILL HAVE COME UP WITH SOME ANSWERS. SOMETIMES I THINK HE'S THE SMARTEST GUY ON THE--
WHAM!
GUTEN ABEND!
WHAT SORCERY IS THIS?!
ZZZZZZZZZZZZZZZAP

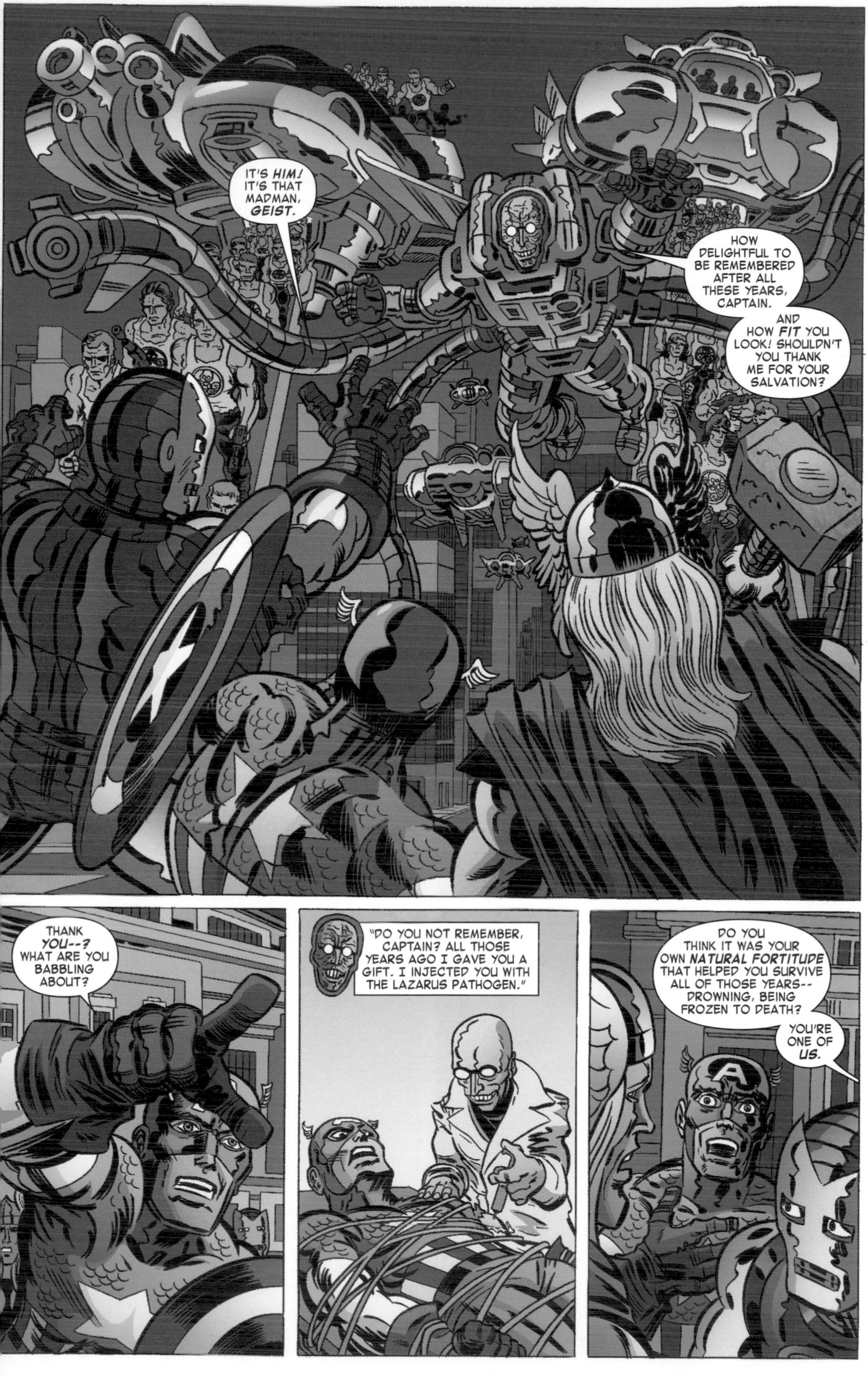
IT'S HIM! IT'S THAT MADMAN, GEIST.
HOW DELIGHTFUL TO BE REMEMBERED AFTER ALL THESE YEARS, CAPTAIN.
AND HOW FIT YOU LOOK! SHOULDN'T YOU THANK ME FOR YOUR SALVATION?
THANK YOU--? WHAT ARE YOU BABBLING ABOUT?
"DO YOU NOT REMEMBER, CAPTAIN? ALL THOSE YEARS AGO I GAVE YOU A GIFT. I INJECTED YOU WITH THE LAZARUS PATHOGEN."
DO YOU THINK IT WAS YOUR OWN NATURAL FORTITUDE THAT HELPED YOU SURVIVE ALL OF THOSE YEARS-- DROWNING, BEING FROZEN TO DEATH?
YOU'RE ONE OF US.

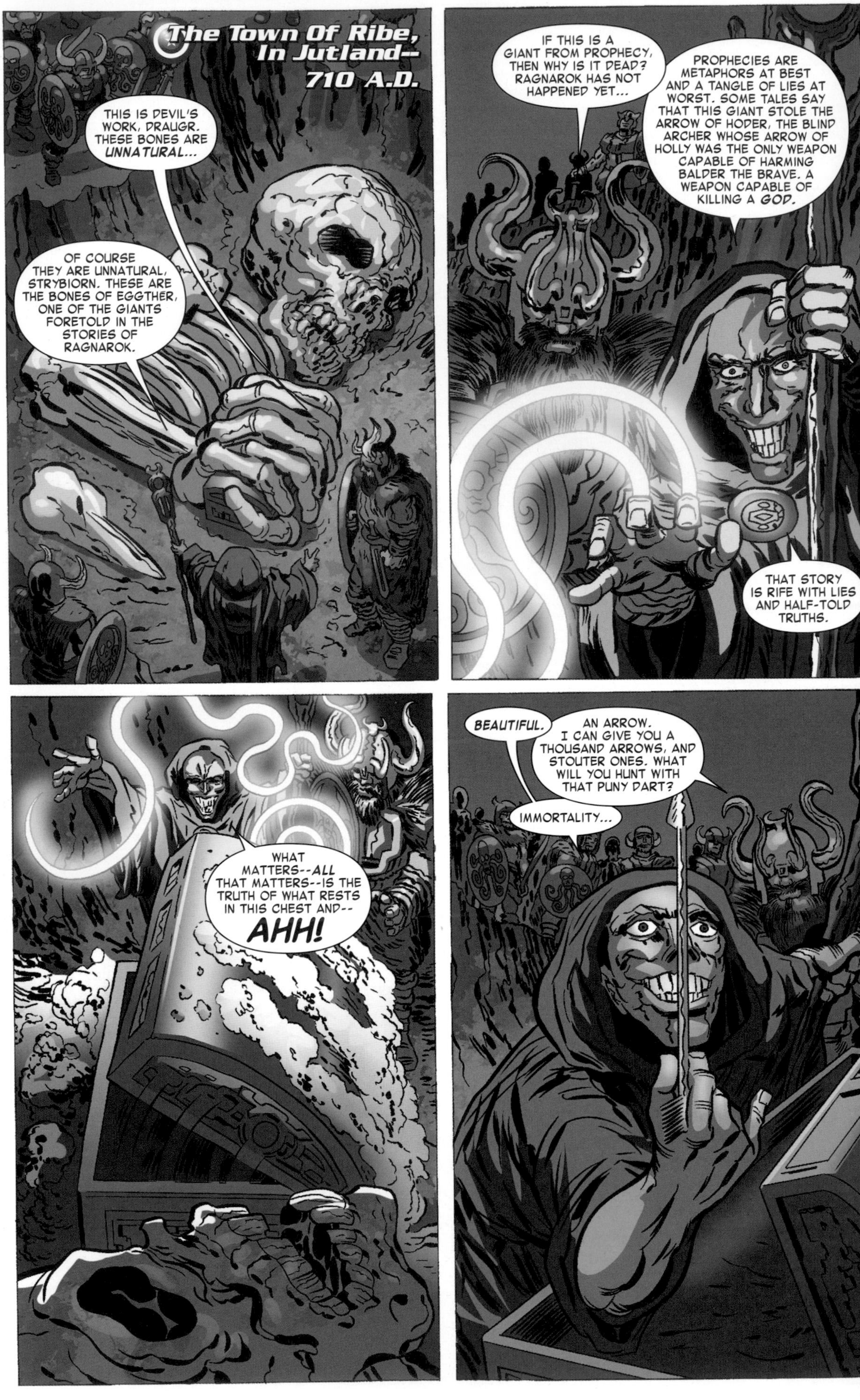
The Town Of Ribe, In Jutland-- 710 A.D.
THIS IS DEVIL'S WORK, DRAUGR. THESE BONES ARE UNNATURAL...
OF COURSE THEY ARE UNNATURAL, STRYBIORN. THESE ARE THE BONES OF EGGTHER, ONE OF THE GIANTS FORETOLD IN THE STORIES OF RAGNAROK.
IF THIS IS A GIANT FROM PROPHECY, THEN WHY IS IT DEAD? RAGNAROK HAS NOT HAPPENED YET...
PROPHECIES ARE METAPHORS AT BEST AND A TANGLE OF LIES AT WORST. SOME TALES SAY THAT THIS GIANT STOLE THE ARROW OF HODER, THE BLIND ARCHER WHOSE ARROW OF HOLLY WAS THE ONLY WEAPON CAPABLE OF HARMING BALDER THE BRAVE. A WEAPON CAPABLE OF KILLING A GOD.
THAT STORY IS RIFE WITH LIES AND HALF-TOLD TRUTHS.
WHAT MATTERS--ALL THAT MATTERS--IS THE TRUTH OF WHAT RESTS IN THIS CHEST AND--
AHH!
BEAUTIFUL.
AN ARROW. I CAN GIVE YOU A THOUSAND ARROWS, AND STOUTER ONES. WHAT WILL YOU HUNT WITH THAT PUNY DART?
IMMORTALITY...

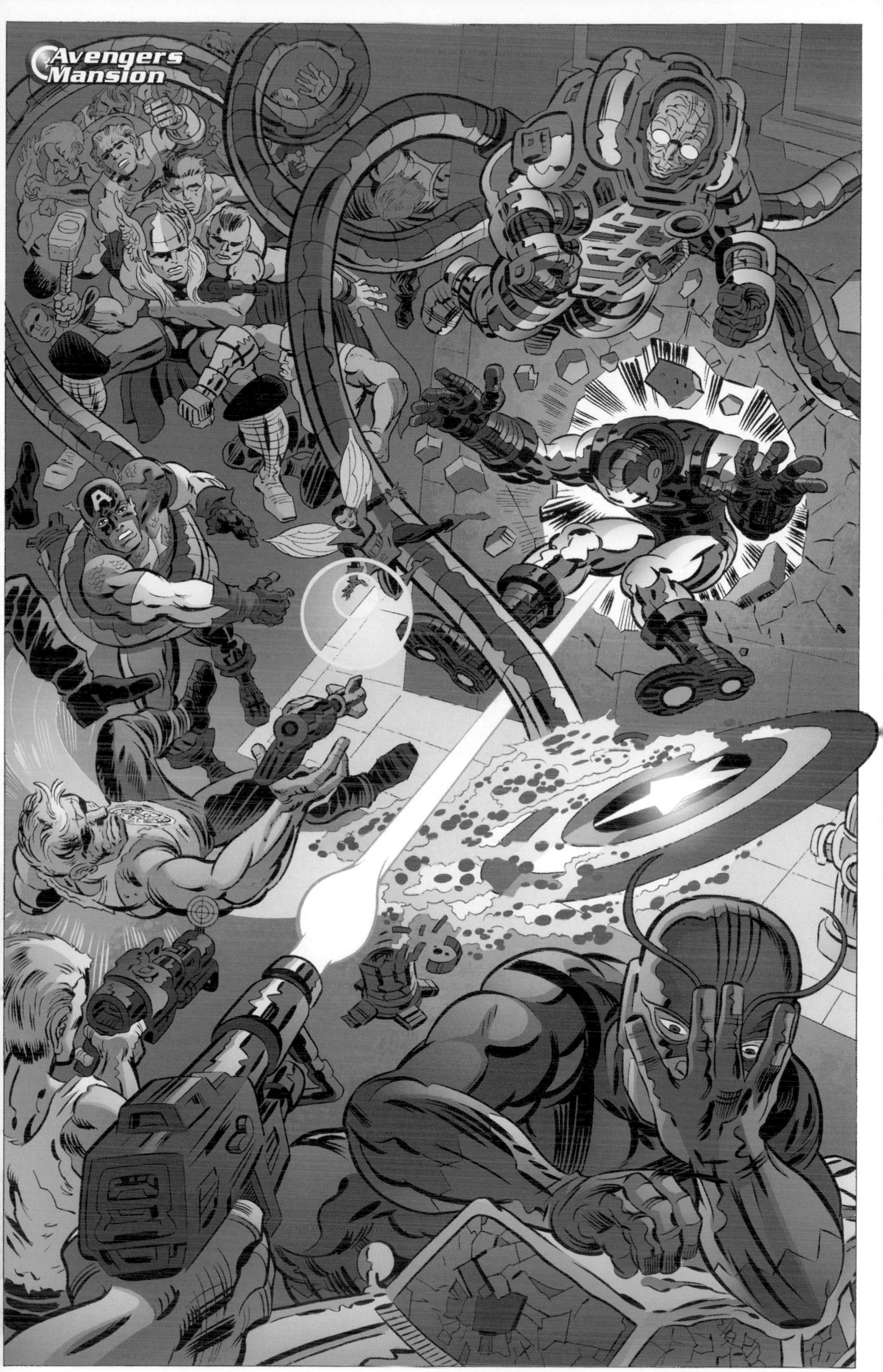
Avengers Mansion

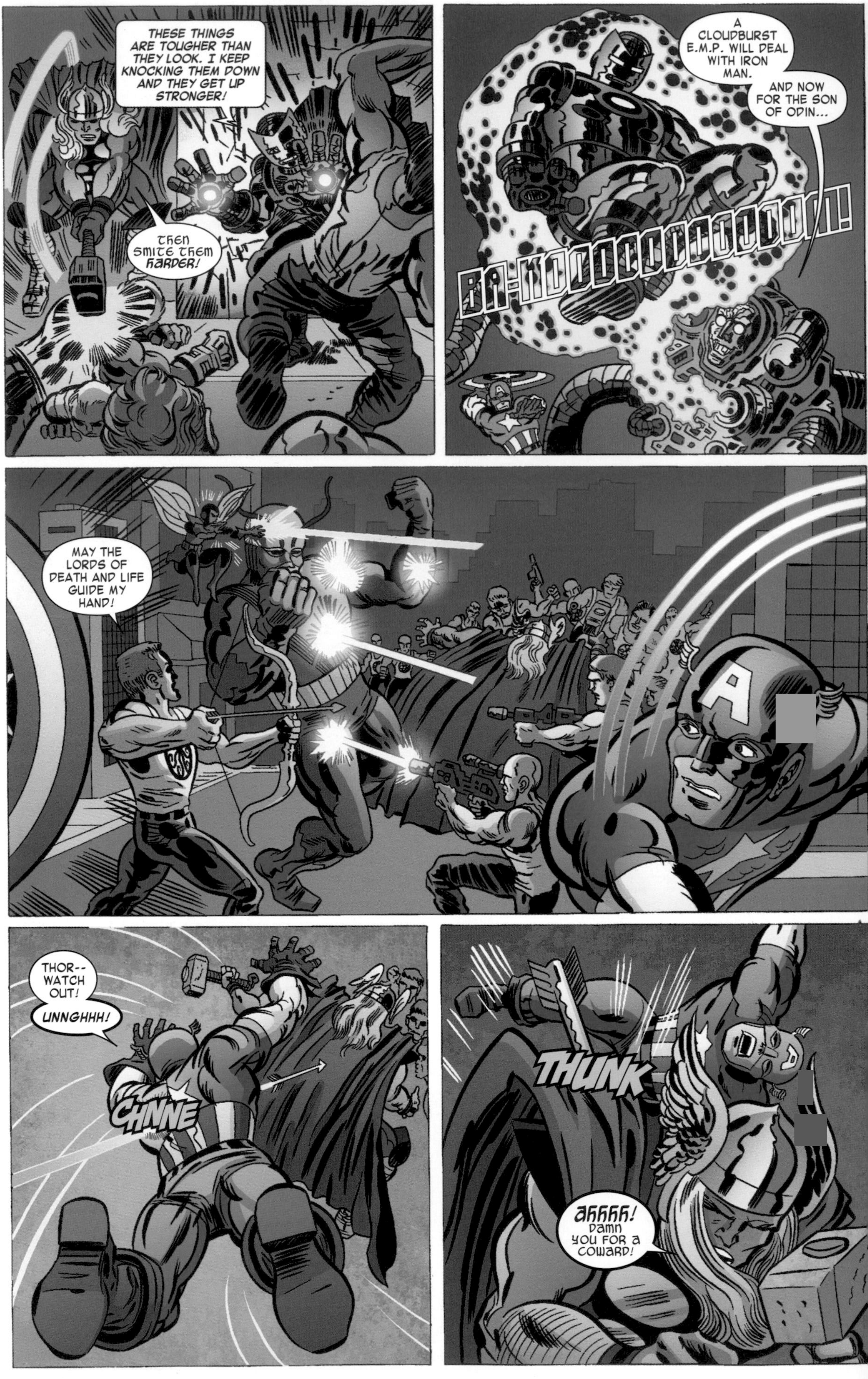
THESE THINGS ARE TOUGHER THAN THEY LOOK. I KEEP KNOCKING THEM DOWN AND THEY GET UP STRONGER!
THEN SMITE THEM HARDER!
A CLOUDBURST E.M.P. WILL DEAL WITH IRON MAN.
AND NOW FOR THE SON OF ODIN...
BA-KOOOOOOOOOOOOOM!
MAY THE LORDS OF DEATH AND LIFE GUIDE MY HAND!
THOR--WATCH OUT!
UNNGHHH!
CHNNE
THUNK
AHHHH! DAMN YOU FOR A COWARD!

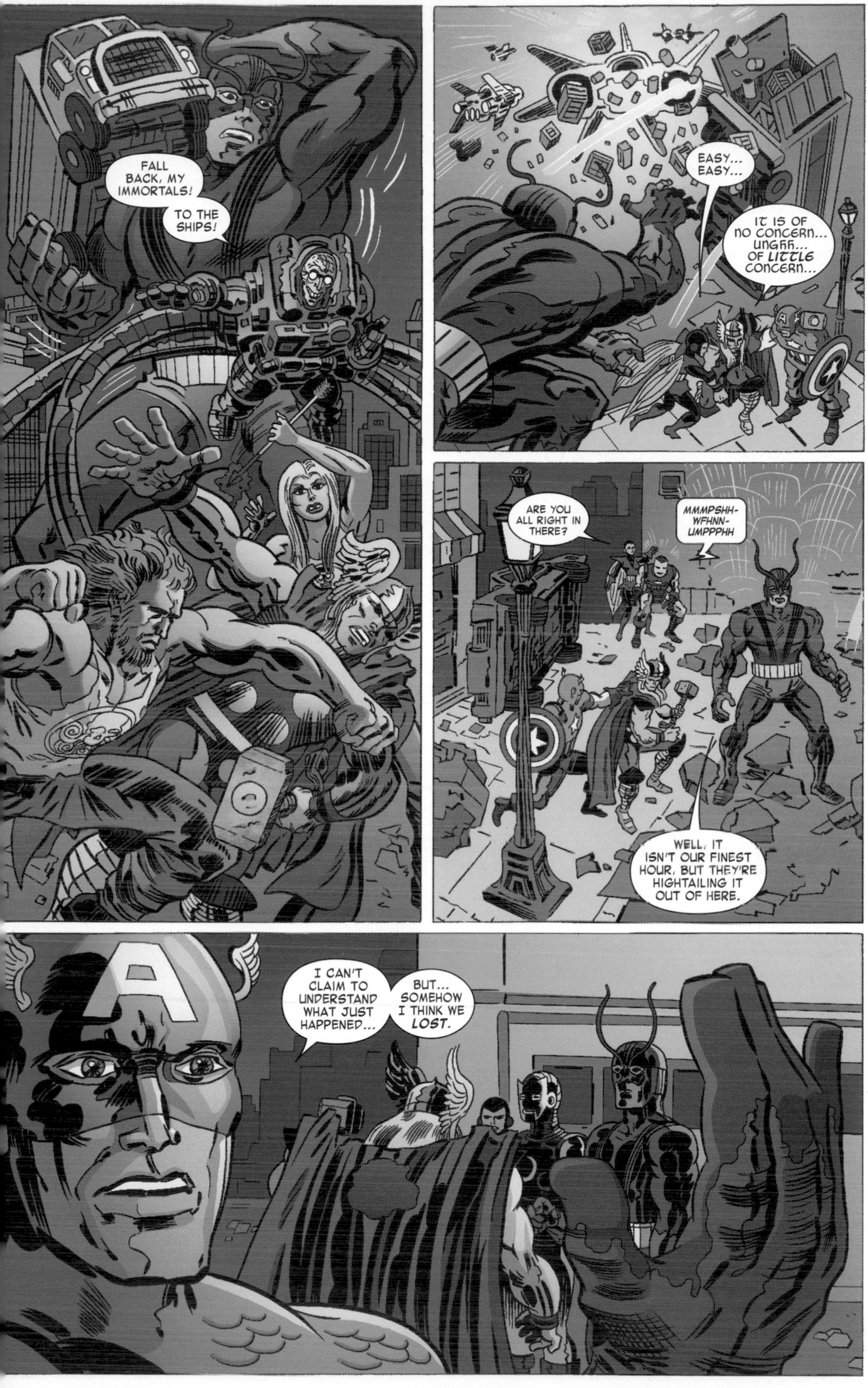
FALL BACK, MY IMMORTALS!
TO THE SHIPS!
EASY... EASY...
IT IS OF NO CONCERN... UNGHH... OF *LITTLE* CONCERN...
ARE YOU ALL RIGHT IN THERE?
MMMPSHH-WFHNN-UMPPPHH
WELL, IT ISN'T OUR FINEST HOUR, BUT THEY'RE HIGHTAILING IT OUT OF HERE.
I CAN'T CLAIM TO UNDERSTAND WHAT JUST HAPPENED...
BUT... SOMEHOW I THINK WE *LOST*.

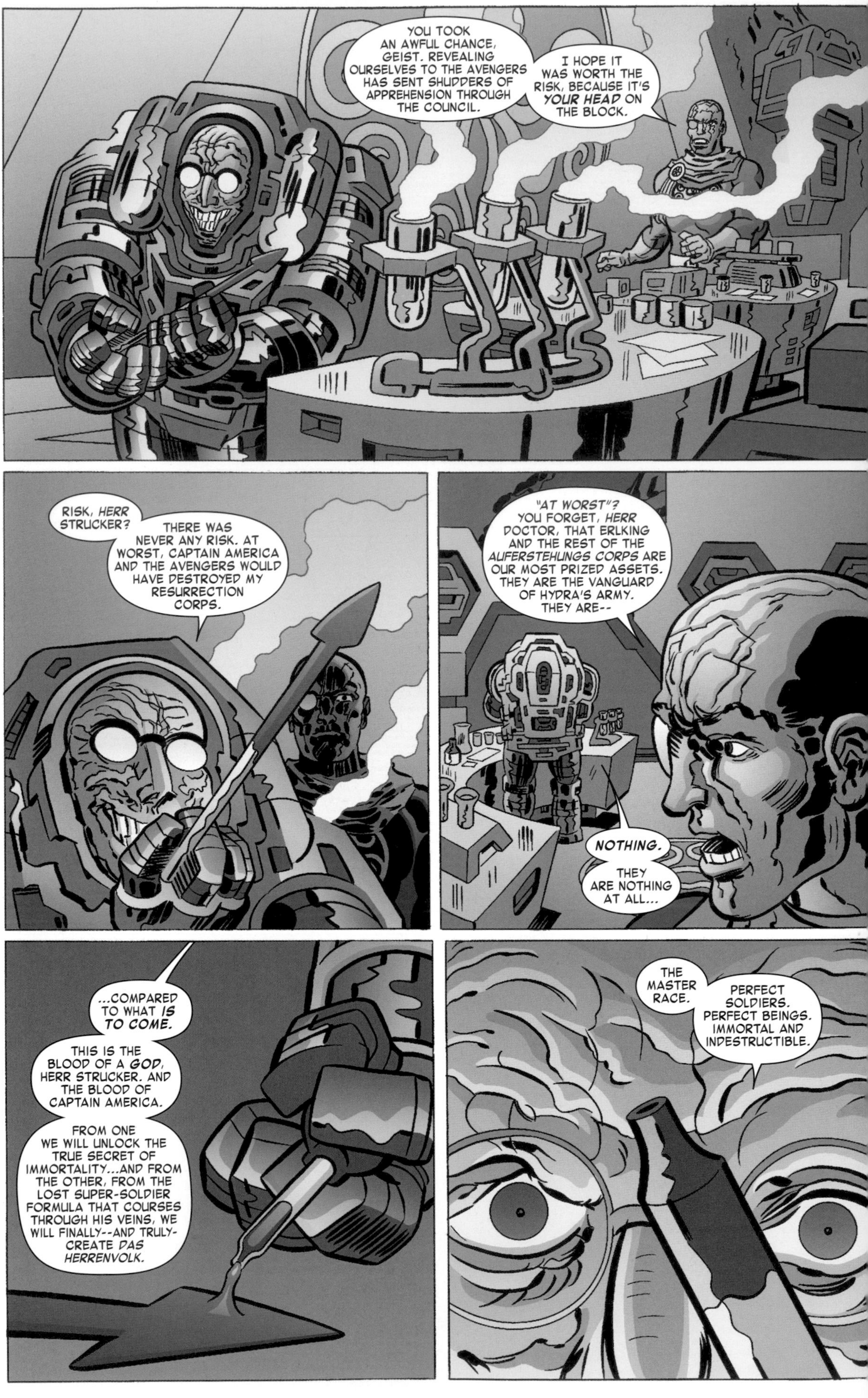
YOU TOOK AN AWFUL CHANCE, GEIST. REVEALING OURSELVES TO THE AVENGERS HAS SENT SHUDDERS OF APPREHENSION THROUGH THE COUNCIL.
I HOPE IT WAS WORTH THE RISK, BECAUSE IT'S *YOUR HEAD* ON THE BLOCK.
RISK, *HERR* STRUCKER?
THERE WAS NEVER ANY RISK. AT WORST, CAPTAIN AMERICA AND THE AVENGERS WOULD HAVE DESTROYED MY RESURRECTION CORPS.
"AT WORST"? YOU FORGET, *HERR* DOCTOR, THAT ERLKING AND THE REST OF THE *AUFERSTEHUNGS CORPS* ARE OUR MOST PRIZED ASSETS. THEY ARE THE VANGUARD OF HYDRA'S ARMY. THEY ARE--
NOTHING.
THEY ARE NOTHING AT ALL...
...COMPARED TO WHAT *IS TO COME.*
THIS IS THE BLOOD OF A *GOD*, HERR STRUCKER. AND THE BLOOD OF CAPTAIN AMERICA.
FROM ONE WE WILL UNLOCK THE TRUE SECRET OF IMMORTALITY...AND FROM THE OTHER, FROM THE LOST SUPER-SOLDIER FORMULA THAT COURSES THROUGH HIS VEINS, WE WILL FINALLY--AND TRULY-CREATE *DAS HERRENVOLK.*
THE MASTER RACE.
PERFECT SOLDIERS. PERFECT BEINGS. IMMORTAL AND INDESTRUCTIBLE.

CAPTAIN AMERICA: HAIL HYDRA
Part 2

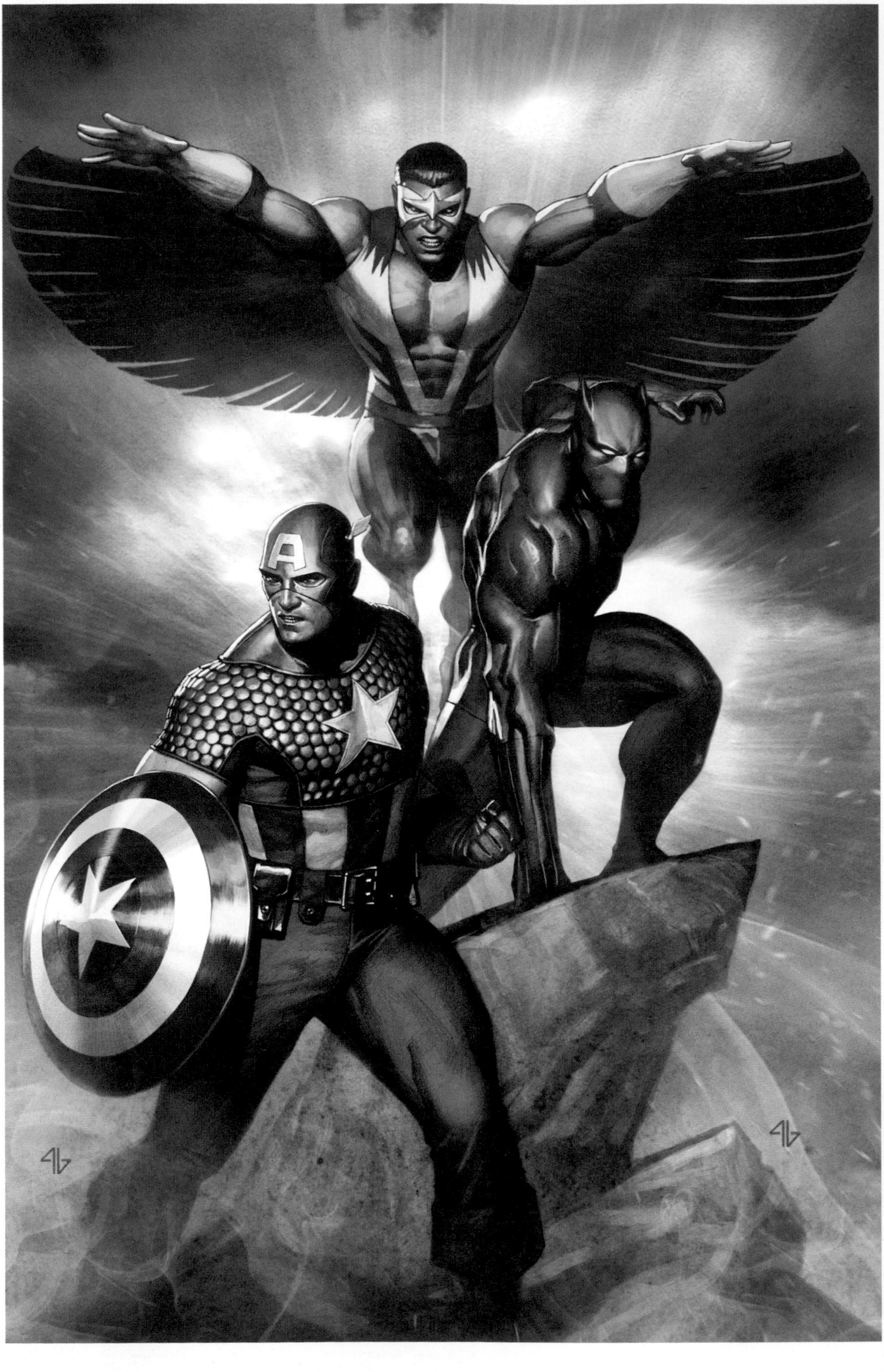

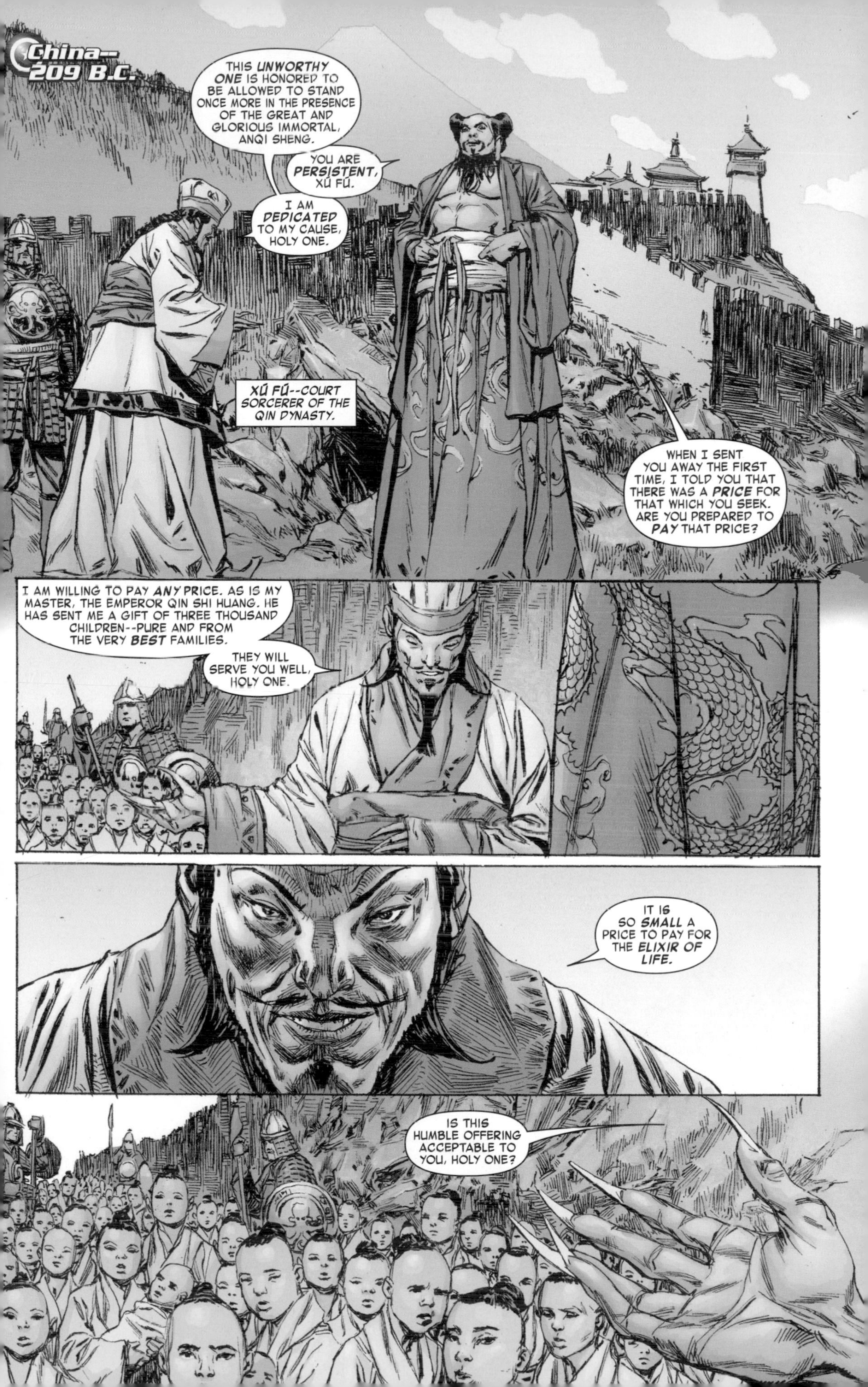
China-- 209 B.C.
THIS UNWORTHY ONE IS HONORED TO BE ALLOWED TO STAND ONCE MORE IN THE PRESENCE OF THE GREAT AND GLORIOUS IMMORTAL, ANQI SHENG.
YOU ARE PERSISTENT, XÚ FÚ.
I AM DEDICATED TO MY CAUSE, HOLY ONE.
XÚ FÚ--COURT SORCERER OF THE QIN DYNASTY.
WHEN I SENT YOU AWAY THE FIRST TIME, I TOLD YOU THAT THERE WAS A PRICE FOR THAT WHICH YOU SEEK. ARE YOU PREPARED TO PAY THAT PRICE?
I AM WILLING TO PAY ANY PRICE. AS IS MY MASTER, THE EMPEROR QIN SHI HUANG. HE HAS SENT ME A GIFT OF THREE THOUSAND CHILDREN--PURE AND FROM THE VERY BEST FAMILIES.
THEY WILL SERVE YOU WELL, HOLY ONE.
IT IS SO SMALL A PRICE TO PAY FOR THE ELIXIR OF LIFE.
IS THIS HUMBLE OFFERING ACCEPTABLE TO YOU, HOLY ONE?

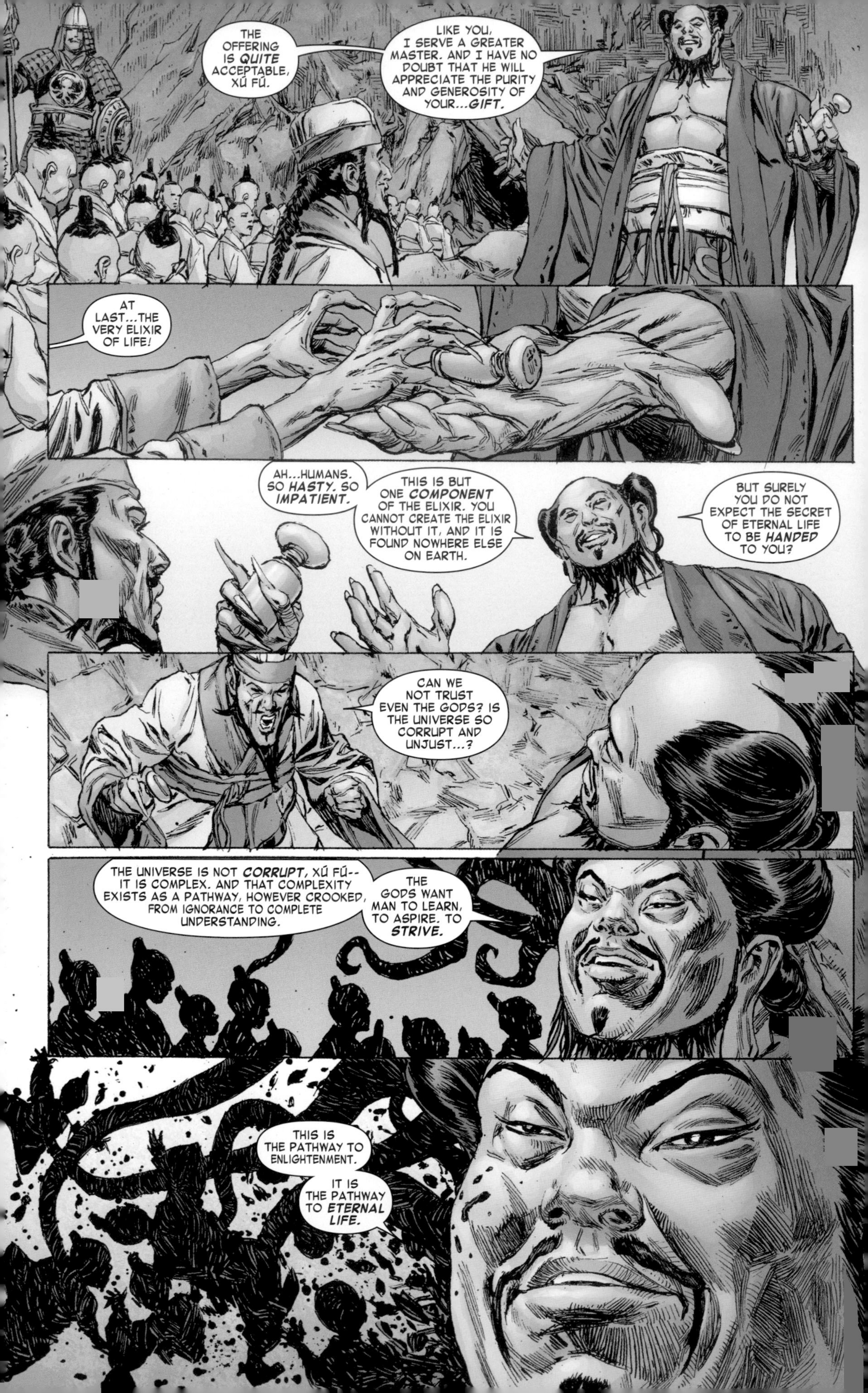
THE OFFERING IS *QUITE* ACCEPTABLE, XÚ FÚ.
LIKE YOU, I SERVE A GREATER MASTER. AND I HAVE NO DOUBT THAT HE WILL APPRECIATE THE PURITY AND GENEROSITY OF YOUR...*GIFT.*
AT LAST...THE VERY ELIXIR OF LIFE!
AH...HUMANS. SO *HASTY.* SO *IMPATIENT.*
THIS IS BUT ONE *COMPONENT* OF THE ELIXIR. YOU CANNOT CREATE THE ELIXIR WITHOUT IT, AND IT IS FOUND NOWHERE ELSE ON EARTH.
BUT SURELY YOU DO NOT EXPECT THE SECRET OF ETERNAL LIFE TO BE *HANDED* TO YOU?
CAN WE NOT TRUST EVEN THE GODS? IS THE UNIVERSE SO CORRUPT AND UNJUST...?
THE UNIVERSE IS NOT *CORRUPT,* XÚ FÚ--IT IS COMPLEX. AND THAT COMPLEXITY EXISTS AS A PATHWAY, HOWEVER CROOKED, FROM IGNORANCE TO COMPLETE UNDERSTANDING.
THE GODS WANT MAN TO LEARN, TO ASPIRE. TO *STRIVE.*
THIS IS THE PATHWAY TO ENLIGHTENMENT.
IT IS THE PATHWAY TO *ETERNAL LIFE.*

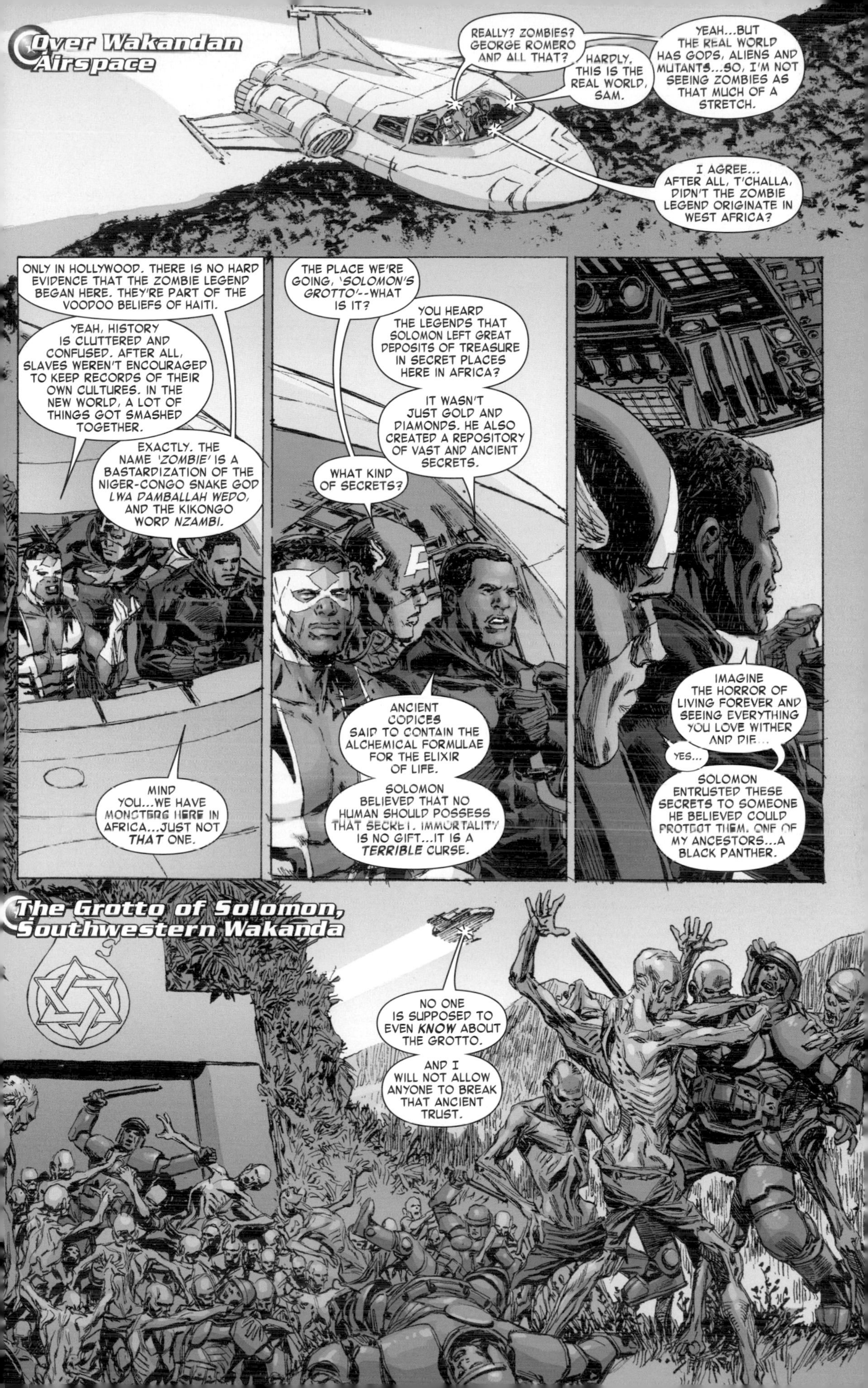

Over Wakandan Airspace
REALLY? ZOMBIES? GEORGE ROMERO AND ALL THAT?
HARDLY. THIS IS THE REAL WORLD, SAM.
YEAH...BUT THE REAL WORLD HAS GODS, ALIENS AND MUTANTS...SO, I'M NOT SEEING ZOMBIES AS THAT MUCH OF A STRETCH.
I AGREE... AFTER ALL, T'CHALLA, DIDN'T THE ZOMBIE LEGEND ORIGINATE IN WEST AFRICA?
ONLY IN HOLLYWOOD. THERE IS NO HARD EVIDENCE THAT THE ZOMBIE LEGEND BEGAN HERE. THEY'RE PART OF THE VOODOO BELIEFS OF HAITI.
YEAH, HISTORY IS CLUTTERED AND CONFUSED. AFTER ALL, SLAVES WEREN'T ENCOURAGED TO KEEP RECORDS OF THEIR OWN CULTURES. IN THE NEW WORLD, A LOT OF THINGS GOT SMASHED TOGETHER.
EXACTLY. THE NAME 'ZOMBIE' IS A BASTARDIZATION OF THE NIGER-CONGO SNAKE GOD LWA DAMBALLAH WEDO, AND THE KIKONGO WORD NZAMBI.
MIND YOU...WE HAVE MONSTERS HERE IN AFRICA...JUST NOT THAT ONE.
THE PLACE WE'RE GOING, 'SOLOMON'S GROTTO'--WHAT IS IT?
YOU HEARD THE LEGENDS THAT SOLOMON LEFT GREAT DEPOSITS OF TREASURE IN SECRET PLACES HERE IN AFRICA?
IT WASN'T JUST GOLD AND DIAMONDS. HE ALSO CREATED A REPOSITORY OF VAST AND ANCIENT SECRETS.
WHAT KIND OF SECRETS?
ANCIENT CODICES SAID TO CONTAIN THE ALCHEMICAL FORMULAE FOR THE ELIXIR OF LIFE.
SOLOMON BELIEVED THAT NO HUMAN SHOULD POSSESS THAT SECRET. IMMORTALITY IS NO GIFT...IT IS A TERRIBLE CURSE.
IMAGINE THE HORROR OF LIVING FOREVER AND SEEING EVERYTHING YOU LOVE WITHER AND DIE...
YES...
SOLOMON ENTRUSTED THESE SECRETS TO SOMEONE HE BELIEVED COULD PROTECT THEM. ONE OF MY ANCESTORS...A BLACK PANTHER.
The Grotto of Solomon, Southwestern Wakanda
NO ONE IS SUPPOSED TO EVEN KNOW ABOUT THE GROTTO.
AND I WILL NOT ALLOW ANYONE TO BREAK THAT ANCIENT TRUST.

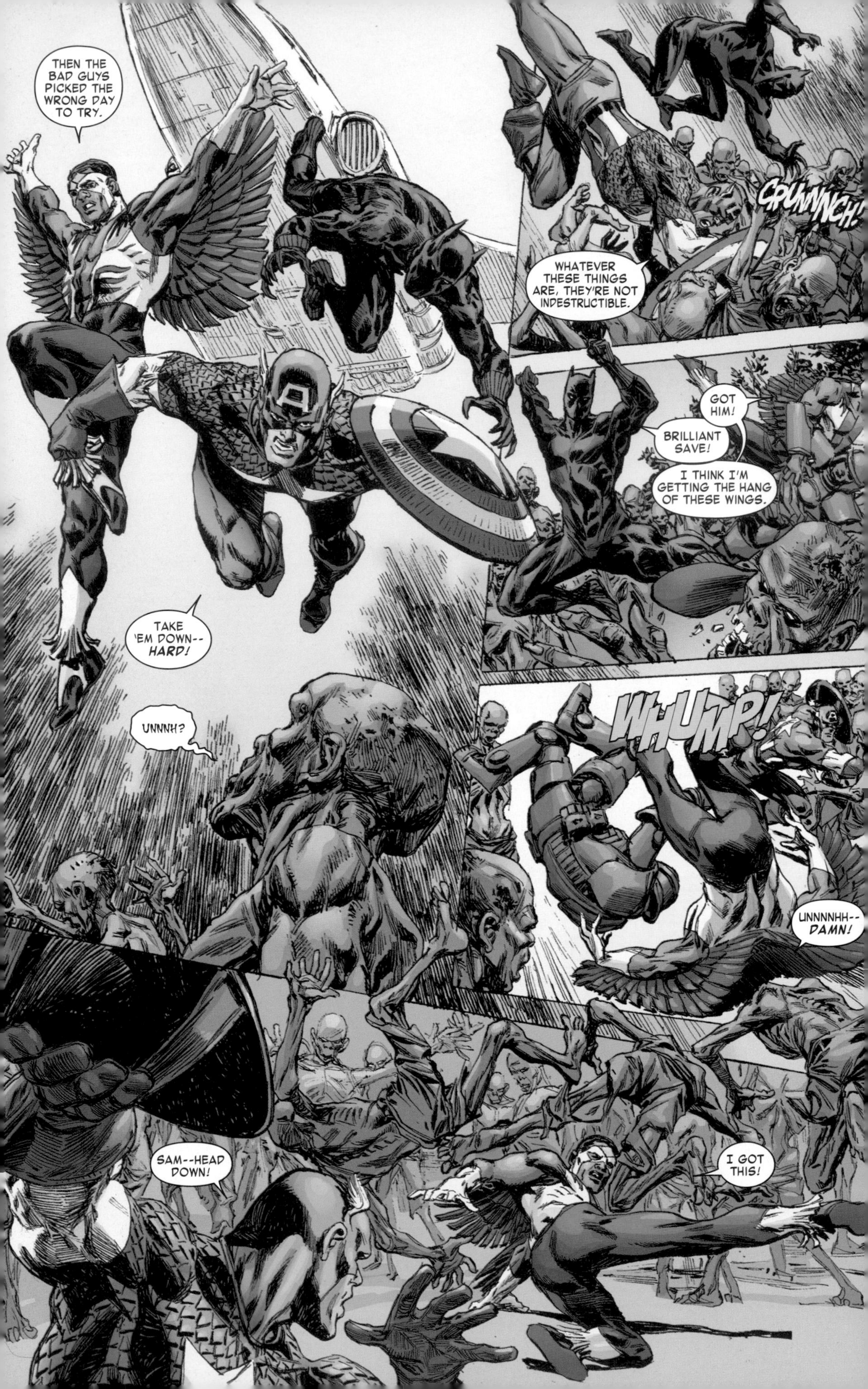
THEN THE BAD GUYS PICKED THE WRONG DAY TO TRY.
TAKE 'EM DOWN--HARD!
CRUNNNCH!
WHATEVER THESE THINGS ARE, THEY'RE NOT INDESTRUCTIBLE.
GOT HIM!
BRILLIANT SAVE!
I THINK I'M GETTING THE HANG OF THESE WINGS.
UNNNH?
WHUMP!
UNNNNHH--DAMN!
SAM--HEAD DOWN!
I GOT THIS!

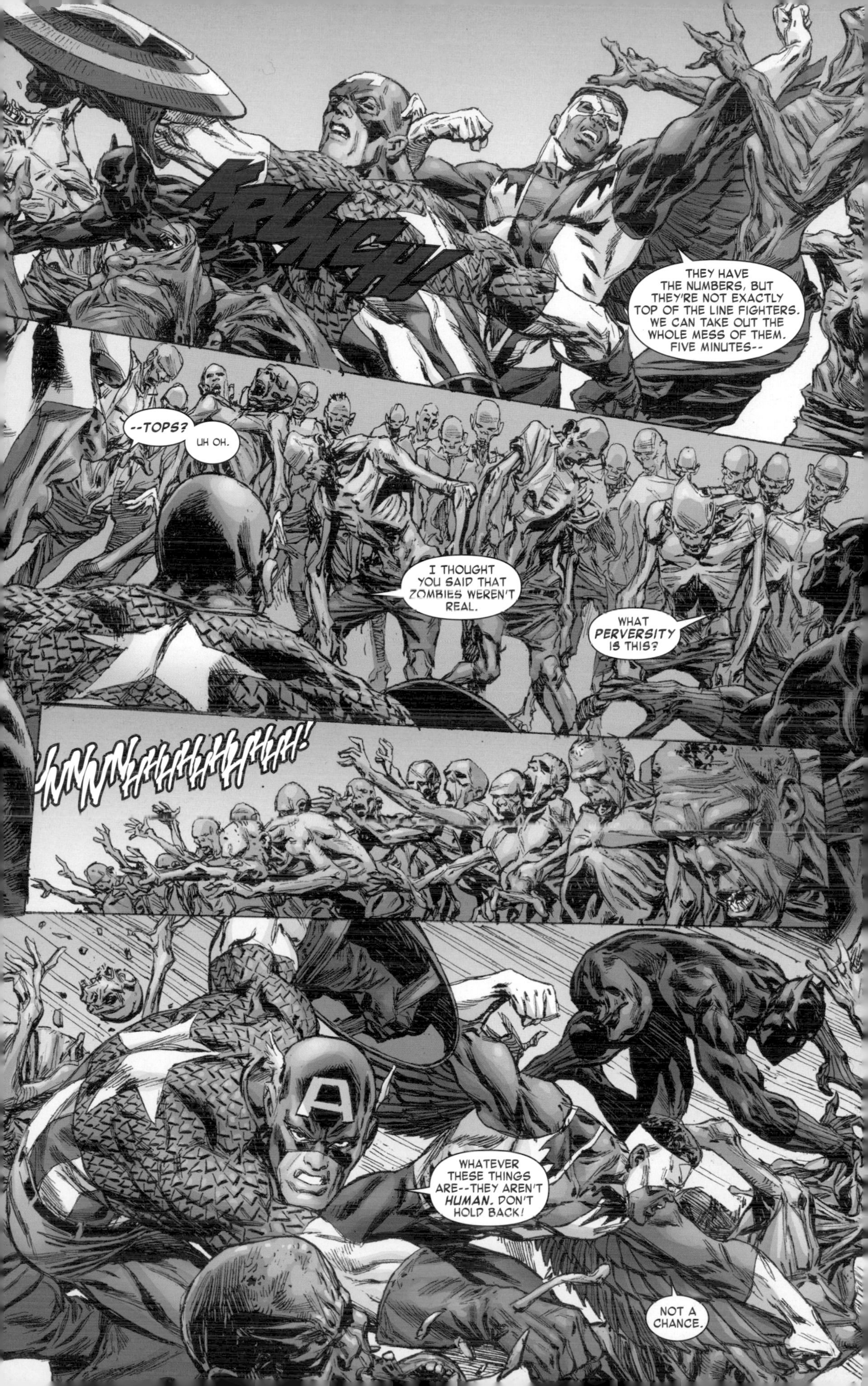
KRUNCH!
THEY HAVE THE NUMBERS, BUT THEY'RE NOT EXACTLY TOP OF THE LINE FIGHTERS. WE CAN TAKE OUT THE WHOLE MESS OF THEM. FIVE MINUTES--
--TOPS?
UH OH.
I THOUGHT YOU SAID THAT ZOMBIES WEREN'T REAL.
WHAT PERVERSITY IS THIS?
HNNNNHHHHHHHHHH!
WHATEVER THESE THINGS ARE--THEY AREN'T HUMAN. DON'T HOLD BACK!
NOT A CHANCE.

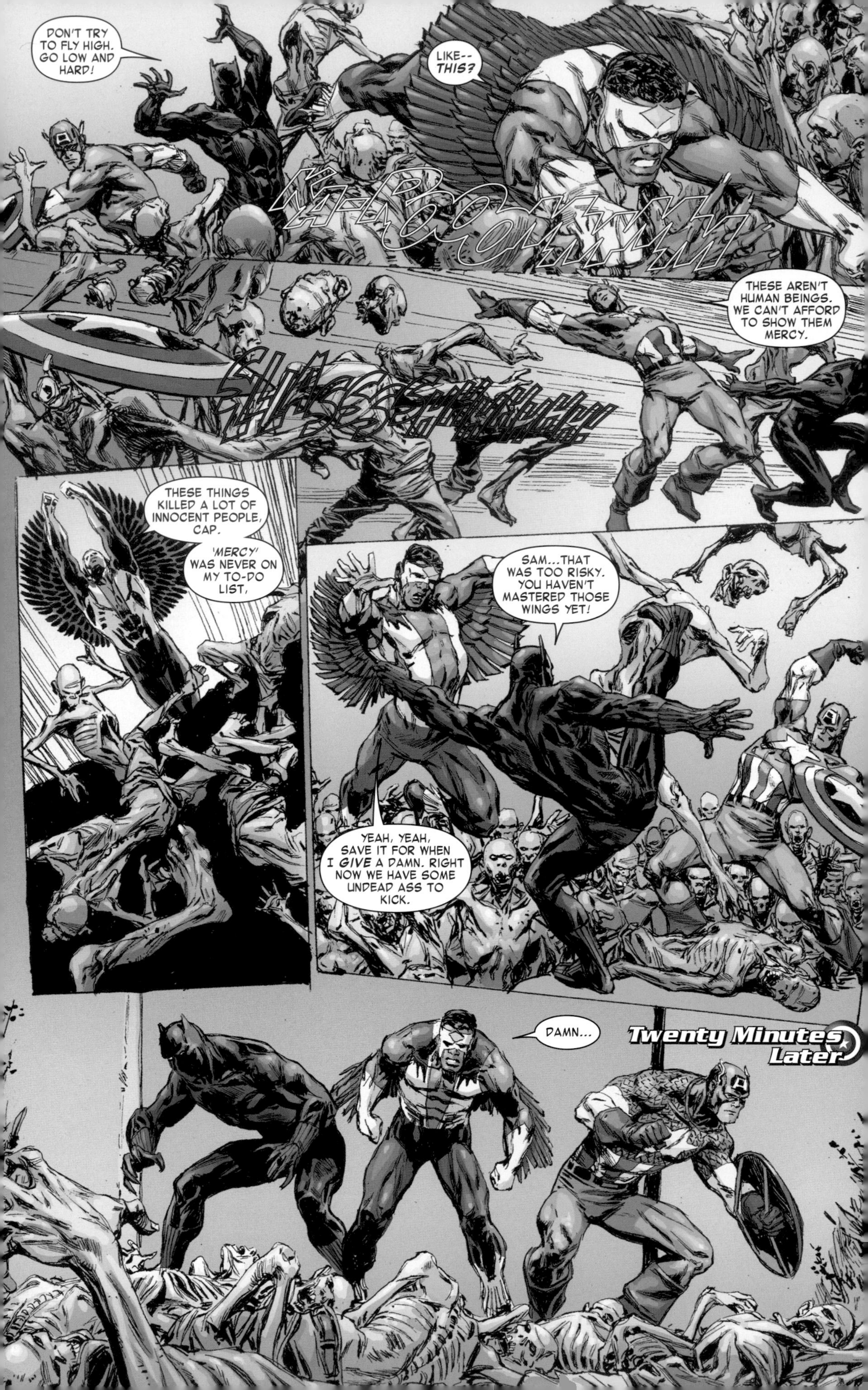
DON'T TRY TO FLY HIGH. GO LOW AND HARD!
LIKE-- THIS?
THESE AREN'T HUMAN BEINGS. WE CAN'T AFFORD TO SHOW THEM MERCY.
THESE THINGS KILLED A LOT OF INNOCENT PEOPLE, CAP.
'MERCY' WAS NEVER ON MY TO-DO LIST.
SAM...THAT WAS TOO RISKY. YOU HAVEN'T MASTERED THOSE WINGS YET!
YEAH, YEAH, SAVE IT FOR WHEN I GIVE A DAMN. RIGHT NOW WE HAVE SOME UNDEAD ASS TO KICK.
Twenty Minutes Later
DAMN...

--BUT THESE WERE ZOMBIES, CAP. NOTHING LIKE THE GERMAN RESURRECTION CORPS WE FOUGHT A FEW YEARS AGO.

TONY STARK-- A.K.A. IRON MAN.

AYE-- THEY WERE ALPS--FIERCE, INTELLIGENT MONSTERS FROM ARYAN LEGENDS.

THOR-- ASGARDIAN GOD OF THUNDER.

I KNOW... BUT WE CAN'T IGNORE THE CONNECTION.

THIS IS A HYDRA OPERATION.

SO THIS IS ABOUT HYDRA TRYING TO CRACK THE SECRET OF IMMORTALITY?

THAT... AND DEFEATING DEATH. TWO AGENDAS WITH SIMILAR AIMS.

WANDA MAXIMOFF-- A.K.A. THE SCARLET WITCH.

BUT... SURELY THE ZOMBIES AND THE RESURRECTION CORPS CAN'T BE THE END GAME. NOT FOR HYDRA. IMMORTALITY WOULDN'T BE WORTH LIVING IF YOU HAD TO BE A MONSTER.

THERE WERE DOZENS OF REFERENCES TO ANCIENT PEOPLE AND PLACES. GILGAMESH, ALEXANDER THE GREAT, ACHILLES, XÚ FÚ...

THESE NAMES ARE ALL TIED TO THE QUEST FOR IMMORTALITY. MANY HAVE MADE SACRIFICES IN THE VAIN HOPE OF RECEIVING THE GIFT OF GODHOOD. MY FATHER ALWAYS SCORNED SUCH REQUESTS.

GODS ARE GODS, AND MEN ARE MEN.

NO. LIKE THE MANY-HEADED HYDRA ITSELF THERE ARE DIFFERENT ASPECTS TO THIS THING.

AN OLD FRIEND OF MINE DIED BRINGING ME CODED RESEARCH NOTES FROM A GERMAN SCIENTIST NAMED HOMLER. HANK PYM SPENT YEARS TRYING TO CRACK THOSE NOTES. HE WAS ONLY PARTLY SUCCESSFUL.

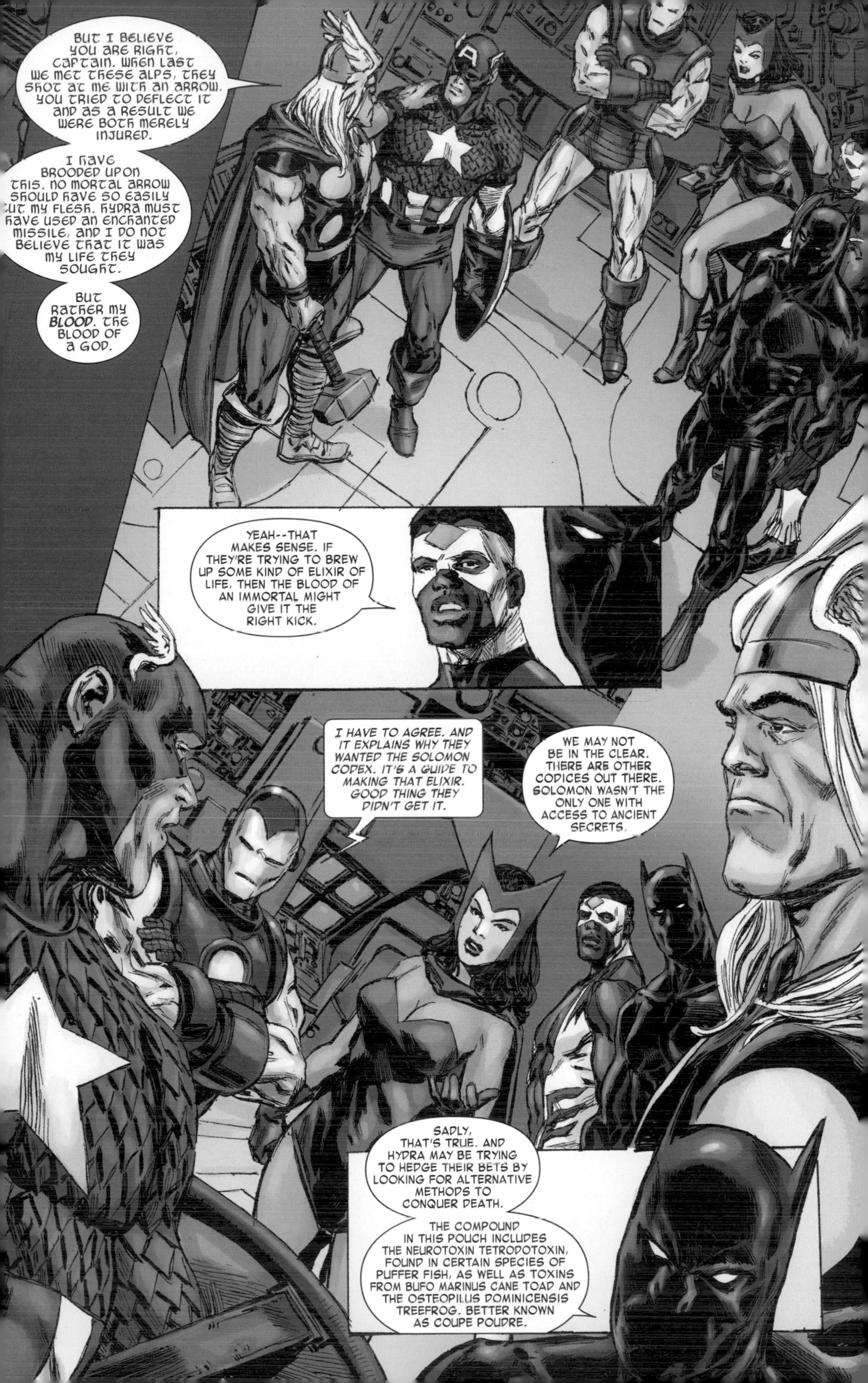

BUT I BELIEVE YOU ARE RIGHT, CAPTAIN. WHEN LAST WE MET THESE ALPS, THEY SHOT AT ME WITH AN ARROW. YOU TRIED TO DEFLECT IT AND AS A RESULT WE WERE BOTH MERELY INJURED.
I HAVE BROODED UPON THIS. NO MORTAL ARROW SHOULD HAVE SO EASILY CUT MY FLESH. HYDRA MUST HAVE USED AN ENCHANTED MISSILE, AND I DO NOT BELIEVE THAT IT WAS MY LIFE THEY SOUGHT.
BUT RATHER MY *BLOOD*. THE BLOOD OF A GOD.
YEAH--THAT MAKES SENSE. IF THEY'RE TRYING TO BREW UP SOME KIND OF ELIXIR OF LIFE, THEN THE BLOOD OF AN IMMORTAL MIGHT GIVE IT THE RIGHT KICK.
I HAVE TO AGREE. AND IT EXPLAINS WHY THEY WANTED THE SOLOMON CODEX. IT'S A GUIDE TO MAKING THAT ELIXIR. GOOD THING THEY DIDN'T GET IT.
WE MAY NOT BE IN THE CLEAR. THERE ARE OTHER CODICES OUT THERE. SOLOMON WASN'T THE ONLY ONE WITH ACCESS TO ANCIENT SECRETS.
SADLY, THAT'S TRUE. AND HYDRA MAY BE TRYING TO HEDGE THEIR BETS BY LOOKING FOR ALTERNATIVE METHODS TO CONQUER DEATH.
THE COMPOUND IN THIS POUCH INCLUDES THE NEUROTOXIN TETRODOTOXIN, FOUND IN CERTAIN SPECIES OF PUFFER FISH, AS WELL AS TOXINS FROM BUFO MARINUS CANE TOAD AND THE OSTEOPILUS DOMINICENSIS TREEFROG. BETTER KNOWN AS COUPE POUDRE.

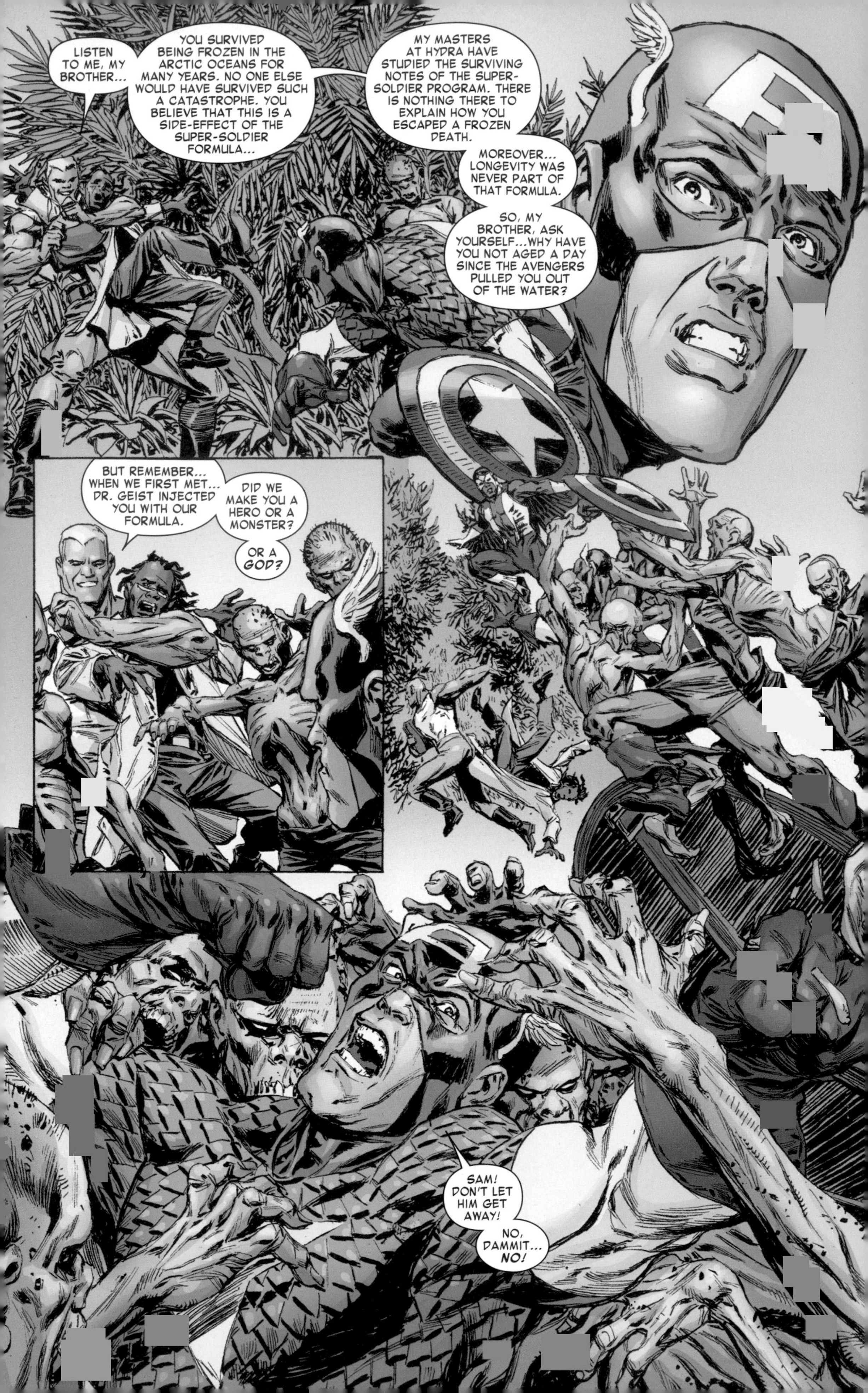
LISTEN TO ME, MY BROTHER...
YOU SURVIVED BEING FROZEN IN THE ARCTIC OCEANS FOR MANY YEARS. NO ONE ELSE WOULD HAVE SURVIVED SUCH A CATASTROPHE. YOU BELIEVE THAT THIS IS A SIDE-EFFECT OF THE SUPER-SOLDIER FORMULA...
MY MASTERS AT HYDRA HAVE STUDIED THE SURVIVING NOTES OF THE SUPER-SOLDIER PROGRAM. THERE IS NOTHING THERE TO EXPLAIN HOW YOU ESCAPED A FROZEN DEATH.
MOREOVER... LONGEVITY WAS NEVER PART OF THAT FORMULA.
SO, MY BROTHER, ASK YOURSELF...WHY HAVE YOU NOT AGED A DAY SINCE THE AVENGERS PULLED YOU OUT OF THE WATER?
BUT REMEMBER... WHEN WE FIRST MET... DR. GEIST INJECTED YOU WITH OUR FORMULA.
DID WE MAKE YOU A HERO OR A MONSTER?
OR A *GOD?*
SAM! DON'T LET HIM GET AWAY!
NO, DAMMIT... *NO!*

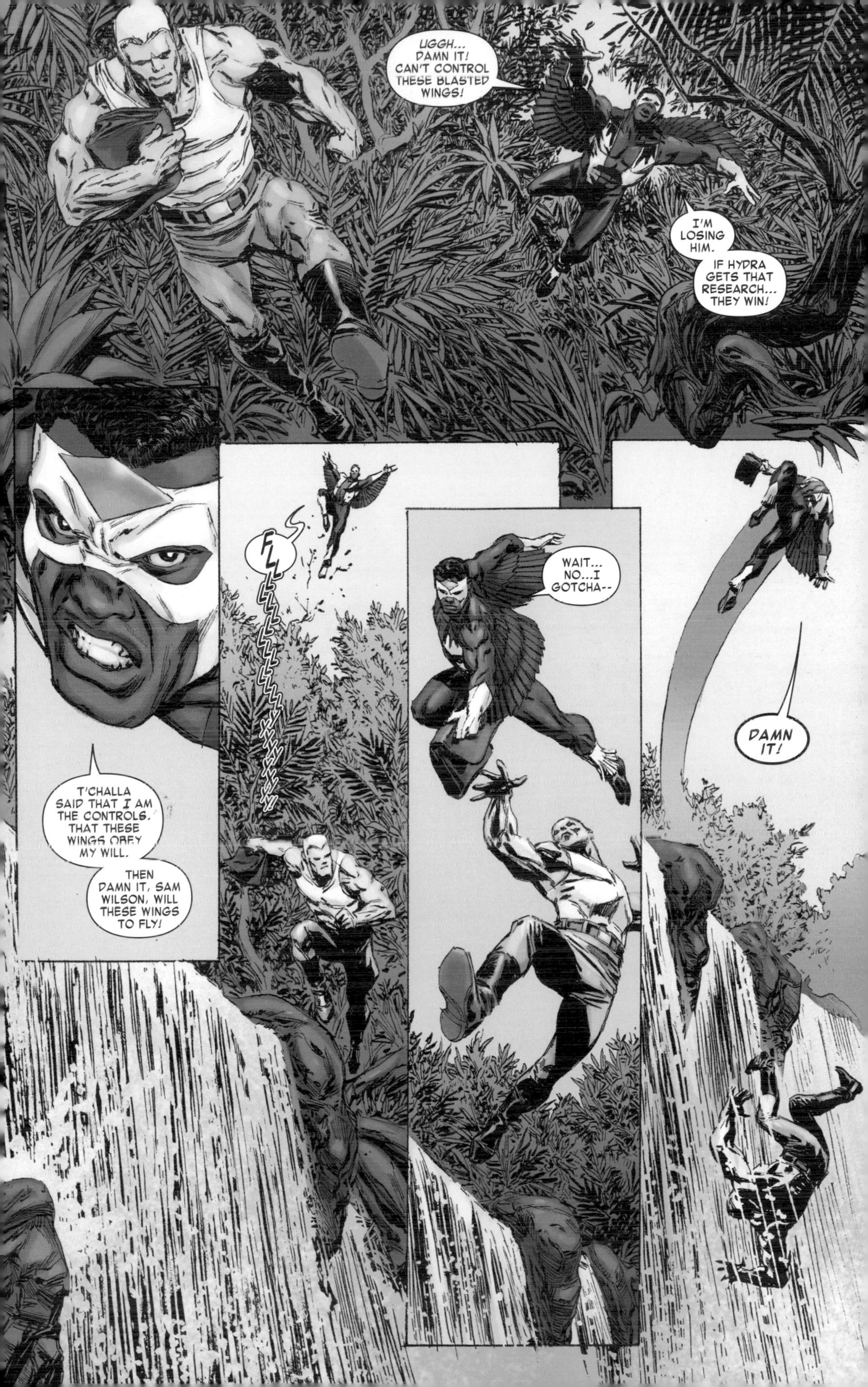
UGGH... DAMN IT! CAN'T CONTROL THESE BLASTED WINGS!
I'M LOSING HIM.
IF HYDRA GETS THAT RESEARCH... THEY WIN!
T'CHALLA SAID THAT I AM THE CONTROLS. THAT THESE WINGS OBEY MY WILL.
THEN DAMN IT, SAM WILSON, WILL THESE WINGS TO FLY!
FLLLLLLLLLYYYYYY
WAIT... NO...I GOTCHA--
DAMN IT!

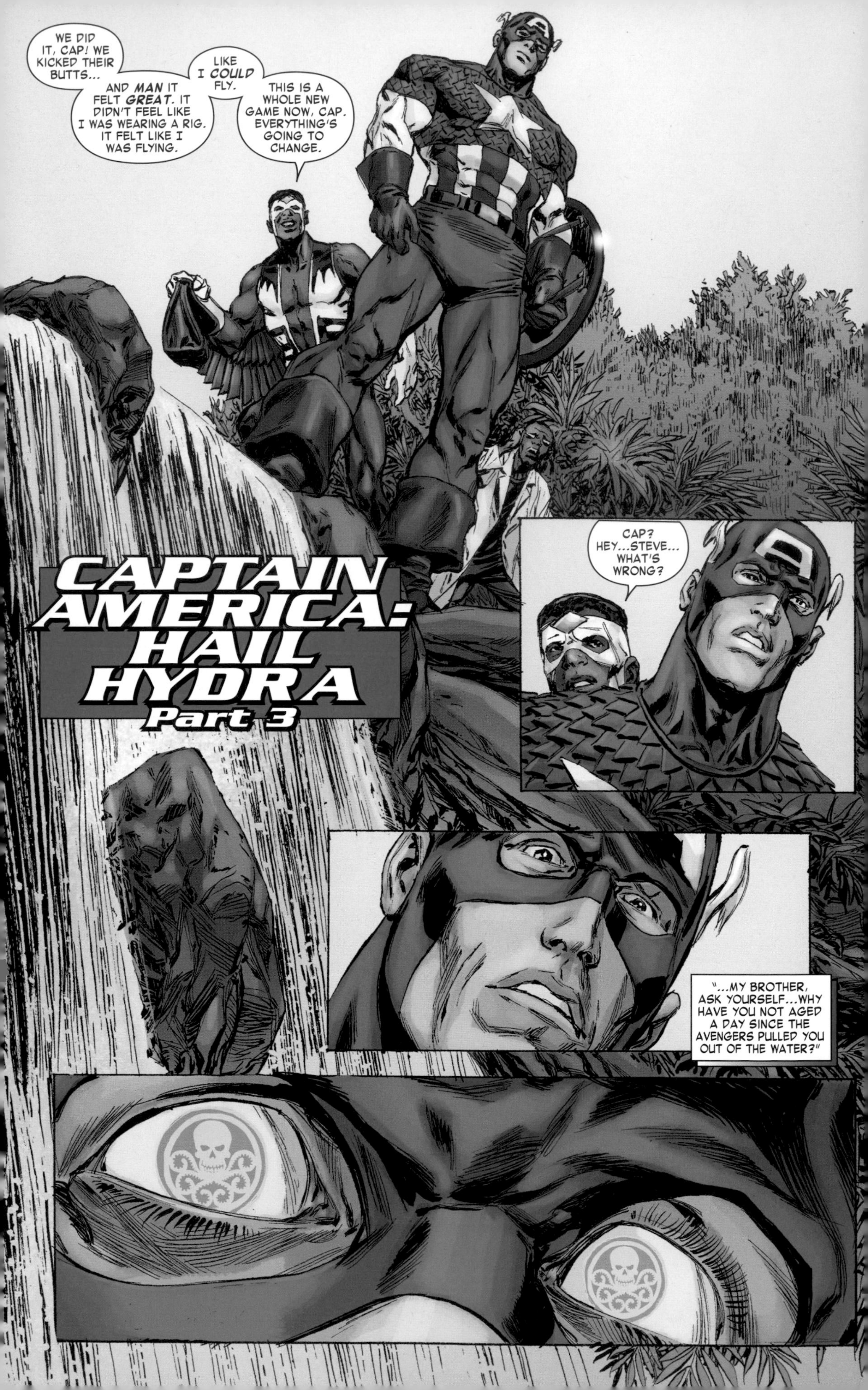
WE DID IT, CAP! WE KICKED THEIR BUTTS...
AND MAN IT FELT GREAT. IT DIDN'T FEEL LIKE I WAS WEARING A RIG. IT FELT LIKE I WAS FLYING.
LIKE I COULD FLY.
THIS IS A WHOLE NEW GAME NOW, CAP. EVERYTHING'S GOING TO CHANGE.
CAPTAIN AMERICA: HAIL HYDRA
Part 3
CAP? HEY...STEVE... WHAT'S WRONG?
"...MY BROTHER, ASK YOURSELF...WHY HAVE YOU NOT AGED A DAY SINCE THE AVENGERS PULLED YOU OUT OF THE WATER?"

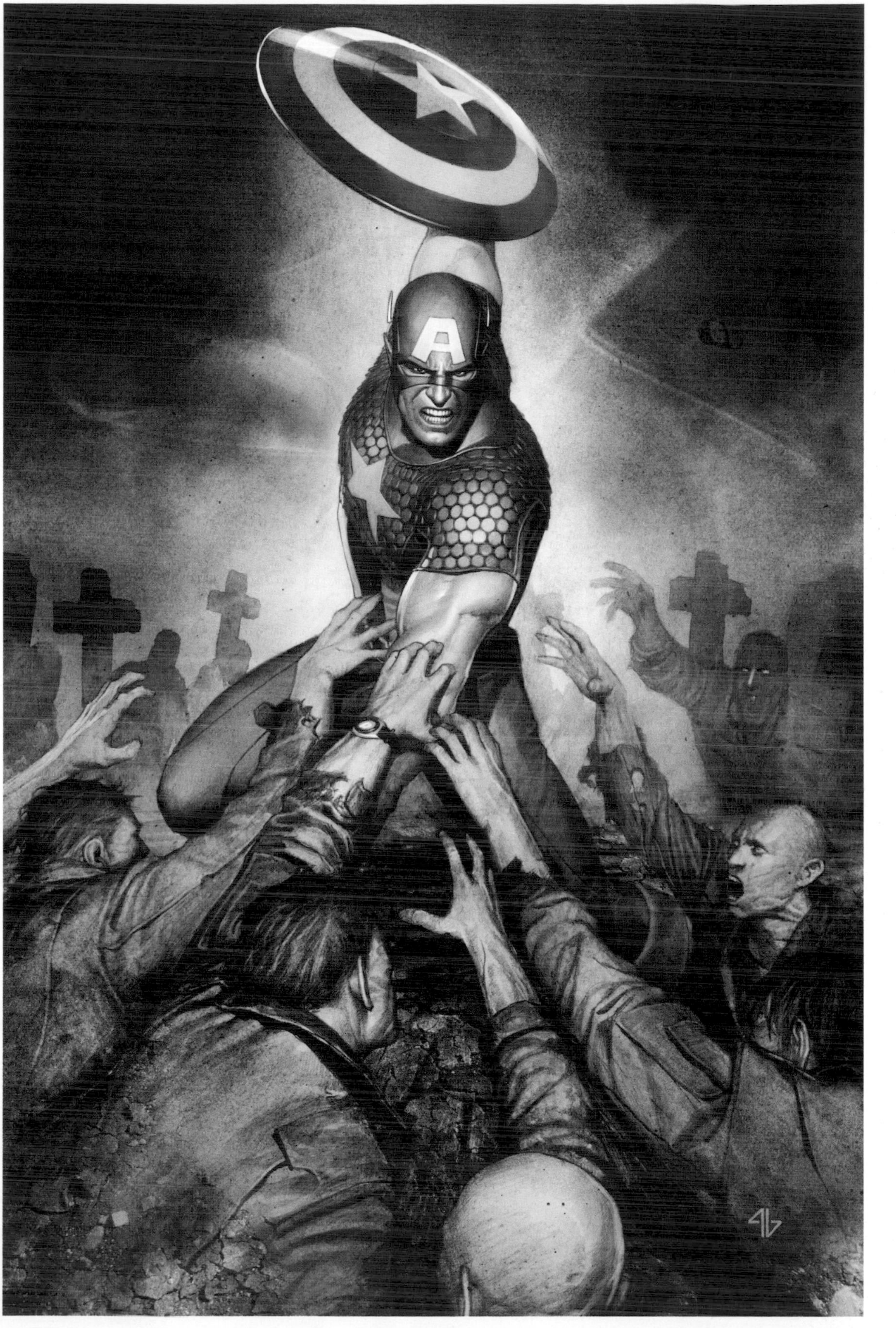

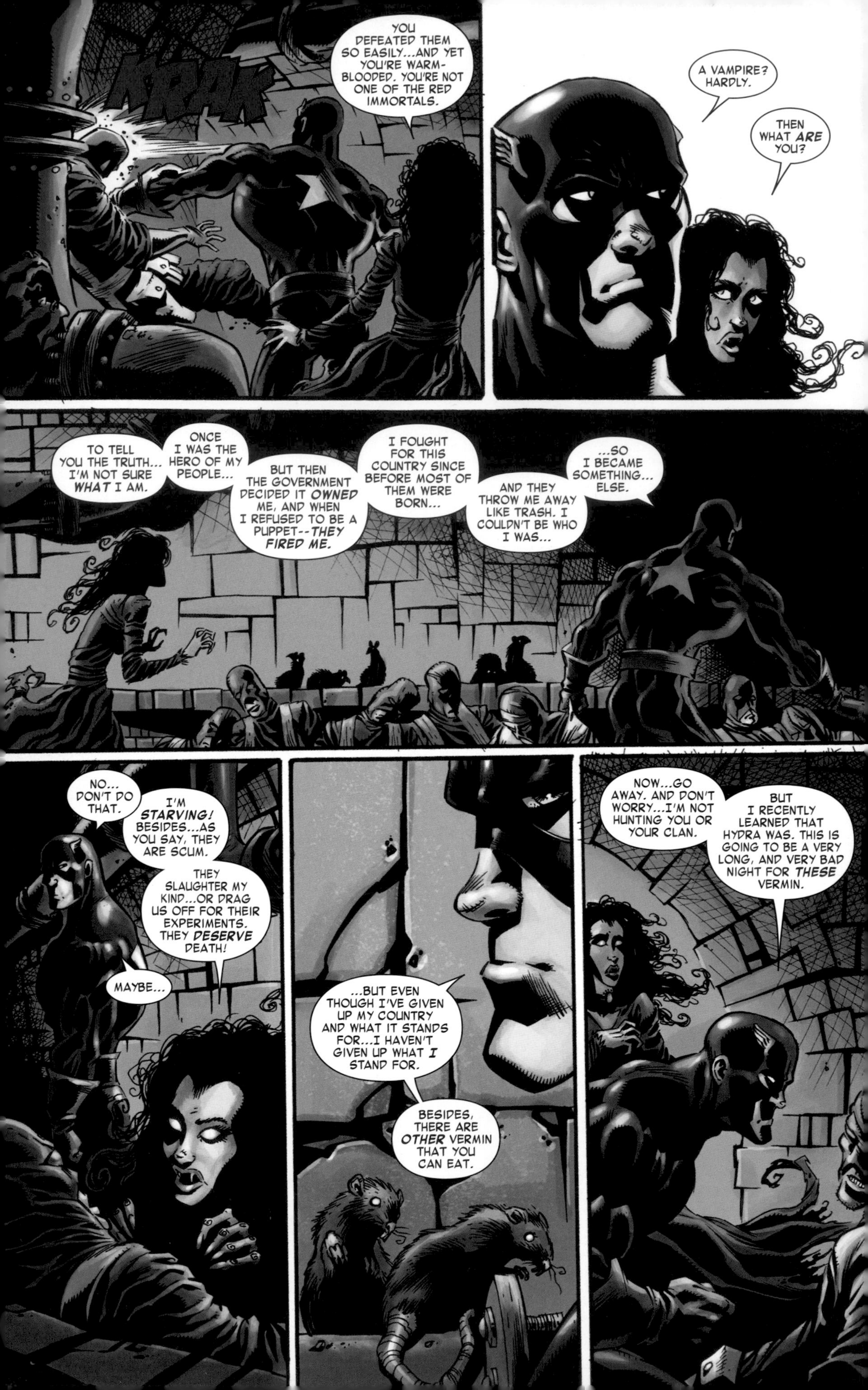
KRAK
YOU DEFEATED THEM SO EASILY...AND YET YOU'RE WARM-BLOODED. YOU'RE NOT ONE OF THE RED IMMORTALS.
A VAMPIRE? HARDLY.
THEN WHAT ARE YOU?
TO TELL YOU THE TRUTH... I'M NOT SURE WHAT I AM.
ONCE I WAS THE HERO OF MY PEOPLE...
BUT THEN THE GOVERNMENT DECIDED IT OWNED ME, AND WHEN I REFUSED TO BE A PUPPET--THEY FIRED ME.
I FOUGHT FOR THIS COUNTRY SINCE BEFORE MOST OF THEM WERE BORN...
AND THEY THROW ME AWAY LIKE TRASH. I COULDN'T BE WHO I WAS...
...SO I BECAME SOMETHING... ELSE.
NO... DON'T DO THAT.
I'M STARVING! BESIDES...AS YOU SAY, THEY ARE SCUM.
THEY SLAUGHTER MY KIND...OR DRAG US OFF FOR THEIR EXPERIMENTS. THEY DESERVE DEATH!
MAYBE...
...BUT EVEN THOUGH I'VE GIVEN UP MY COUNTRY AND WHAT IT STANDS FOR...I HAVEN'T GIVEN UP WHAT I STAND FOR.
BESIDES, THERE ARE OTHER VERMIN THAT YOU CAN EAT.
NOW...GO AWAY. AND DON'T WORRY...I'M NOT HUNTING YOU OR YOUR CLAN.
BUT I RECENTLY LEARNED THAT HYDRA WAS. THIS IS GOING TO BE A VERY LONG, AND VERY BAD NIGHT FOR THESE VERMIN.

HERR STRUCKER... THIS IS A WATERSHED MOMENT.

DR. GEIST-- CHIEF SCIENTIST OF HYDRA'S INFINITAS AGENDA.

THINK OF IT... SIX THOUSAND YEARS OF EXPLORATION AND EXPERIMENTATION. OF DELVING INTO THE DARKEST REGIONS OF MAGIC AND CREATING NEW FIELDS OF SCIENCE...

THE ART OF "ALCHEMY" ITSELF IS LARGELY A BYPRODUCT OF OUR INFINITAS AGENDA. NOW WE ARE APPROACHING THE BRINK!

I AM WITH YOU, HERR GEIST. LIKE YOU, I BURN TO BEHOLD THIS MARVEL...

THE BLOOD OF ACHILLES AND HECTOR, OF THE IMMORTAL THOR, OF THE SUPER-SOLDIER CAPTAIN AMERICA...DNA FROM GODS TO MAKE GIANTS.

DROPS OF THE ELIXIR VITAE... THE RAREST ELEMENTS BROUGHT TOGETHER IN THE MOST COMPLEX POTION EVER ATTEMPTED.

CLANK-A-- CLANK-A-- CLANK--

BEHOLD HIM, STRUCKER. DER UNSTERBLICH!

BARON WOLFGANG VON STRUCKER-- CHIEF OF SPECIAL OPERATIONS FOR HYDRA.

--SO, IT WAS ANOTHER DEAD END?

YES. A WASTE OF TIME AND RESOURCES THAT I DON'T HAVE.

IT'S LIKE I'M CHASING *GHOSTS*.

YOU'RE STIRRING THINGS UP, THOUGH, STEVE. HYDRA HAS A BOUNTY ON YOU BIGGER THAN CANADA'S NATIONAL DEBT.

THE SECRETARY OF STATE WOULD LOVE TO SEE YOUR HEAD ON HIS WALL.

NICK FURY, DIRECTOR OF S.H.I.E.L.D.

NOT A SURPRISE.

NO. YOU WEREN'T MAKING FRIENDS BEFORE YOU DECIDED TO TURN YOURSELF INTO A STATEMENT.

"THE CAPTAIN"? PLEASE. WHY NOT JUST CALL YOURSELF *"CAPTAIN-SHOVE-IT"?*

THIS ISN'T ABOUT ME, NICK, AND IT'S NOT ABOUT POLITICS. THIS IS ABOUT A THREAT TO THE WHOLE WORLD...

...WHICH YOU CAN'T PROVE EVEN *EXISTS*.

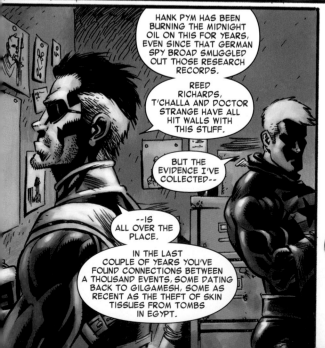

HANK PYM HAS BEEN BURNING THE MIDNIGHT OIL ON THIS FOR YEARS, EVEN SINCE THAT GERMAN SPY BROAD SMUGGLED OUT THOSE RESEARCH RECORDS.

REED RICHARDS, T'CHALLA AND DOCTOR STRANGE HAVE ALL HIT WALLS WITH THIS STUFF.

BUT THE EVIDENCE I'VE COLLECTED--

--IS ALL OVER THE PLACE.

IN THE LAST COUPLE OF YEARS YOU'VE FOUND CONNECTIONS BETWEEN A THOUSAND EVENTS, SOME DATING BACK TO GILGAMESH, SOME AS RECENT AS THE THEFT OF SKIN TISSUES FROM TOMBS IN EGYPT.

DAMN IT--DON'T TELL ME I'M *CRAZY*.

I TOLD YOU WHAT HAPPENED. GEIST INJECTED ME WITH *SOMETHING* BACK IN '44, AND ERLKING HINTED THAT IT WAS THIS *LAZARUS FORMULA* THAT KEPT ME ALIVE IN THE ICE ALL THOSE YEARS.

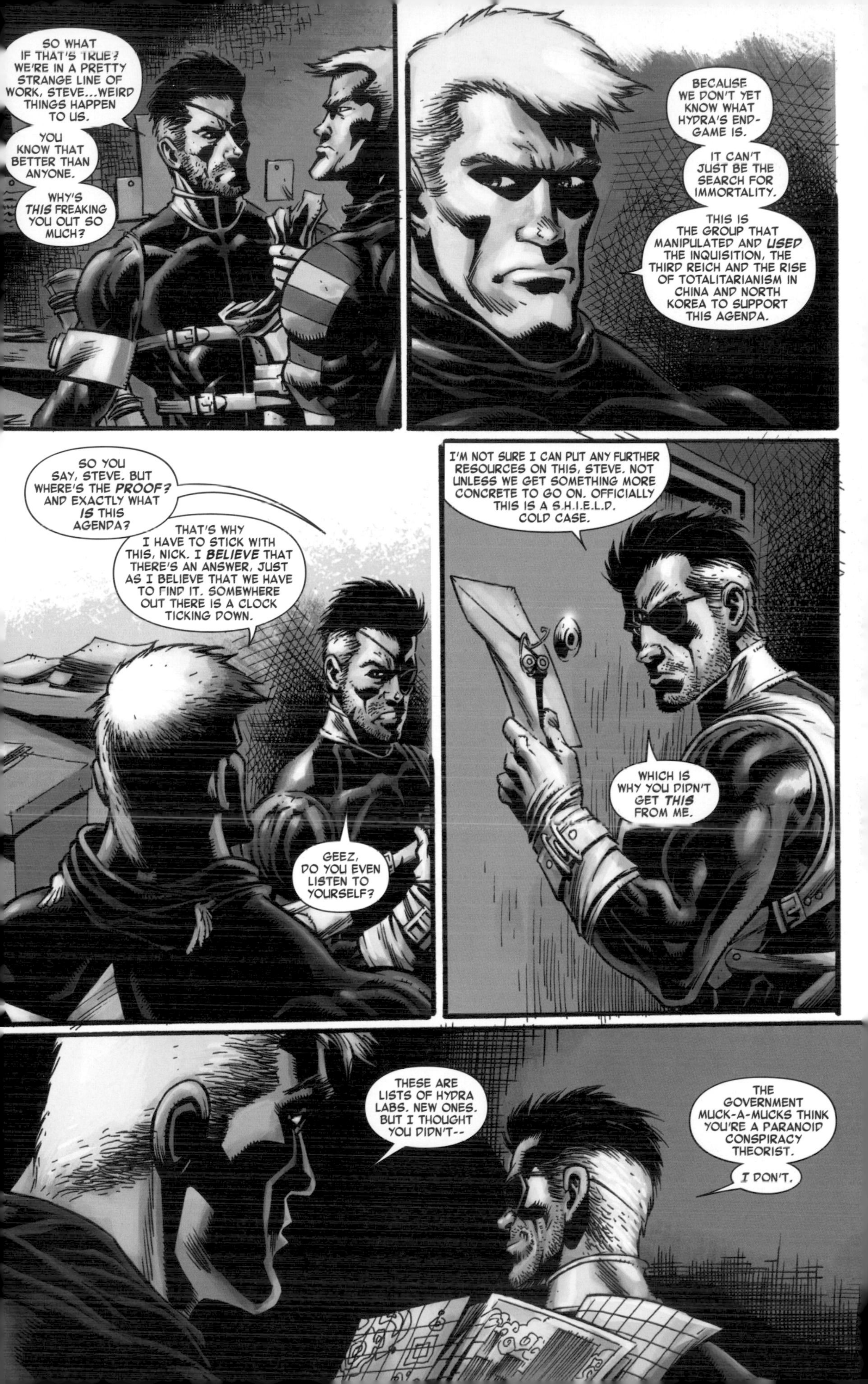
SO WHAT IF THAT'S TRUE? WE'RE IN A PRETTY STRANGE LINE OF WORK, STEVE...WEIRD THINGS HAPPEN TO US.
YOU KNOW THAT BETTER THAN ANYONE.
WHY'S THIS FREAKING YOU OUT SO MUCH?
BECAUSE WE DON'T YET KNOW WHAT HYDRA'S END-GAME IS.
IT CAN'T JUST BE THE SEARCH FOR IMMORTALITY.
THIS IS THE GROUP THAT MANIPULATED AND USED THE INQUISITION, THE THIRD REICH AND THE RISE OF TOTALITARIANISM IN CHINA AND NORTH KOREA TO SUPPORT THIS AGENDA.
SO YOU SAY, STEVE. BUT WHERE'S THE PROOF? AND EXACTLY WHAT IS THIS AGENDA?
THAT'S WHY I HAVE TO STICK WITH THIS, NICK. I BELIEVE THAT THERE'S AN ANSWER, JUST AS I BELIEVE THAT WE HAVE TO FIND IT. SOMEWHERE OUT THERE IS A CLOCK TICKING DOWN.
GEEZ, DO YOU EVEN LISTEN TO YOURSELF?
I'M NOT SURE I CAN PUT ANY FURTHER RESOURCES ON THIS, STEVE. NOT UNLESS WE GET SOMETHING MORE CONCRETE TO GO ON. OFFICIALLY THIS IS A S.H.I.E.L.D. COLD CASE.
WHICH IS WHY YOU DIDN'T GET THIS FROM ME.
THESE ARE LISTS OF HYDRA LABS. NEW ONES. BUT I THOUGHT YOU DIDN'T--
THE GOVERNMENT MUCK-A-MUCKS THINK YOU'RE A PARANOID CONSPIRACY THEORIST.
I DON'T.

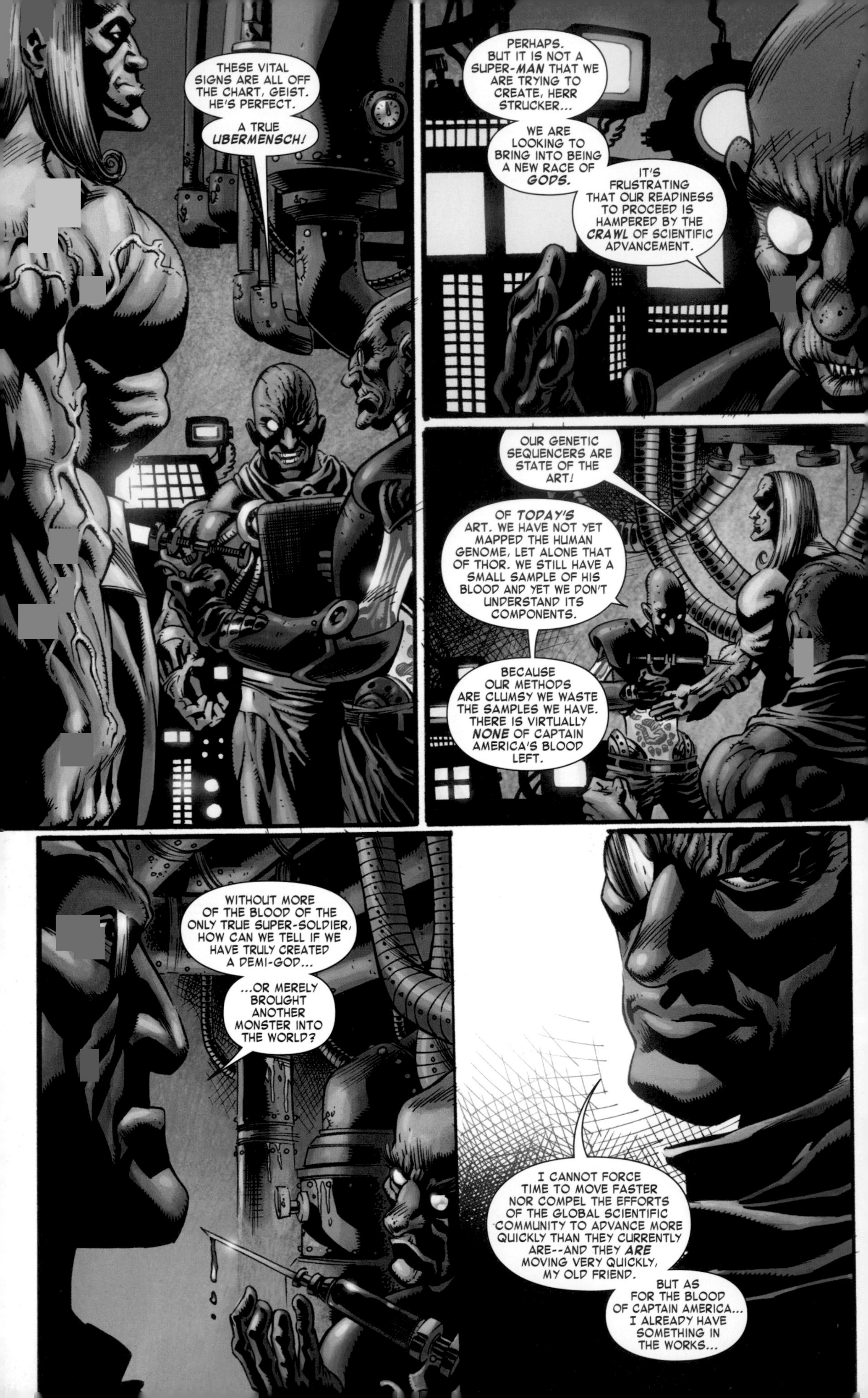
THESE VITAL SIGNS ARE ALL OFF THE CHART, GEIST. HE'S PERFECT.
A TRUE *UBERMENSCH!*
PERHAPS. BUT IT IS NOT A SUPER-*MAN* THAT WE ARE TRYING TO CREATE, HERR STRUCKER...
WE ARE LOOKING TO BRING INTO BEING A NEW RACE OF *GODS.*
IT'S FRUSTRATING THAT OUR READINESS TO PROCEED IS HAMPERED BY THE *CRAWL* OF SCIENTIFIC ADVANCEMENT.
OUR GENETIC SEQUENCERS ARE STATE OF THE ART!
OF *TODAY'S* ART. WE HAVE NOT YET MAPPED THE HUMAN GENOME, LET ALONE THAT OF THOR. WE STILL HAVE A SMALL SAMPLE OF HIS BLOOD AND YET WE DON'T UNDERSTAND ITS COMPONENTS.
BECAUSE OUR METHODS ARE CLUMSY WE WASTE THE SAMPLES WE HAVE. THERE IS VIRTUALLY *NONE* OF CAPTAIN AMERICA'S BLOOD LEFT.
WITHOUT MORE OF THE BLOOD OF THE ONLY TRUE SUPER-SOLDIER, HOW CAN WE TELL IF WE HAVE TRULY CREATED A DEMI-GOD...
...OR MERELY BROUGHT ANOTHER MONSTER INTO THE WORLD?
I CANNOT FORCE TIME TO MOVE FASTER NOR COMPEL THE EFFORTS OF THE GLOBAL SCIENTIFIC COMMUNITY TO ADVANCE MORE QUICKLY THAN THEY CURRENTLY ARE--AND THEY *ARE* MOVING VERY QUICKLY, MY OLD FRIEND.
BUT AS FOR THE BLOOD OF CAPTAIN AMERICA... I ALREADY HAVE SOMETHING IN THE WORKS...

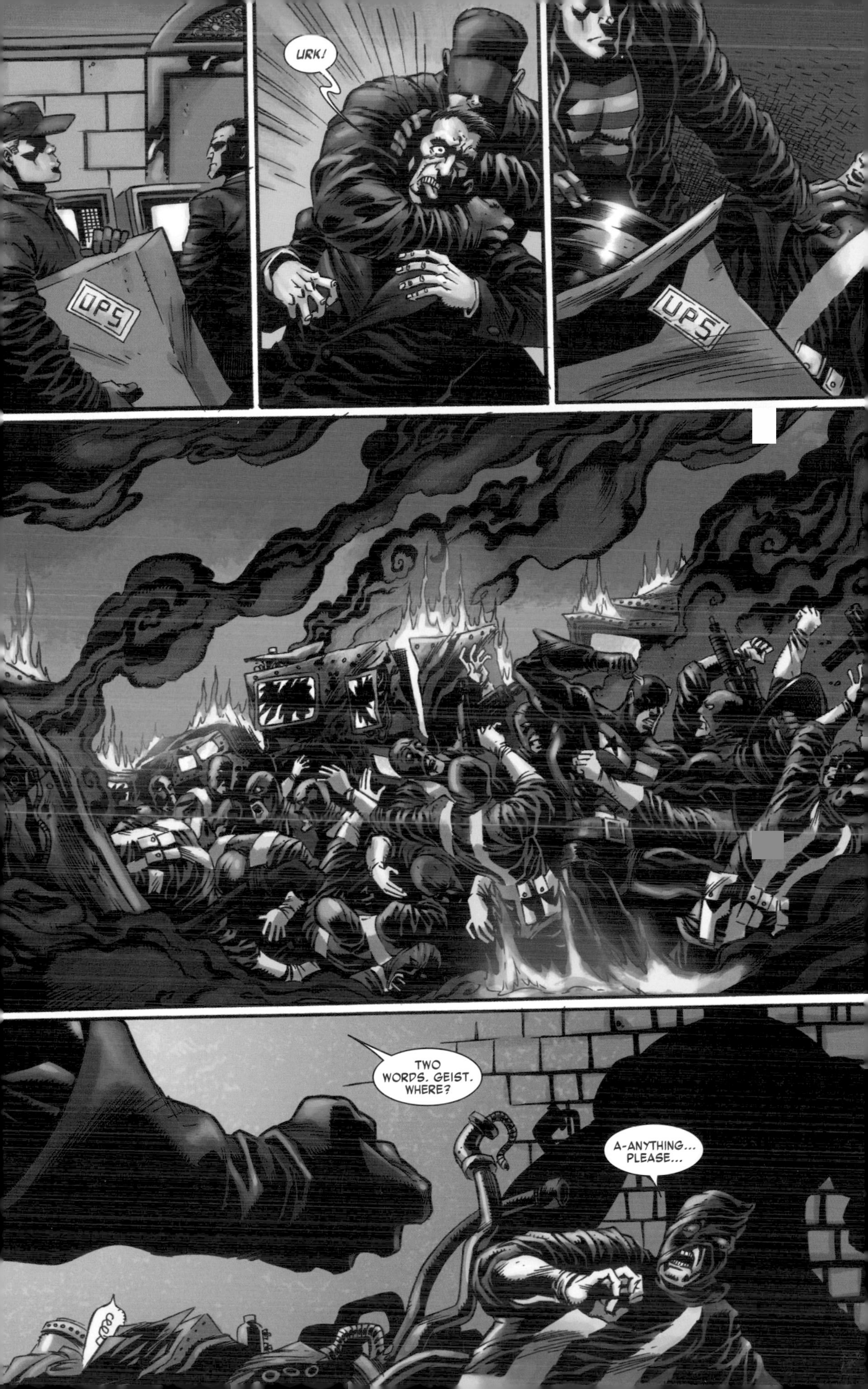
URK!
TWO WORDS. GEIST. WHERE?
A-ANYTHING... PLEASE...

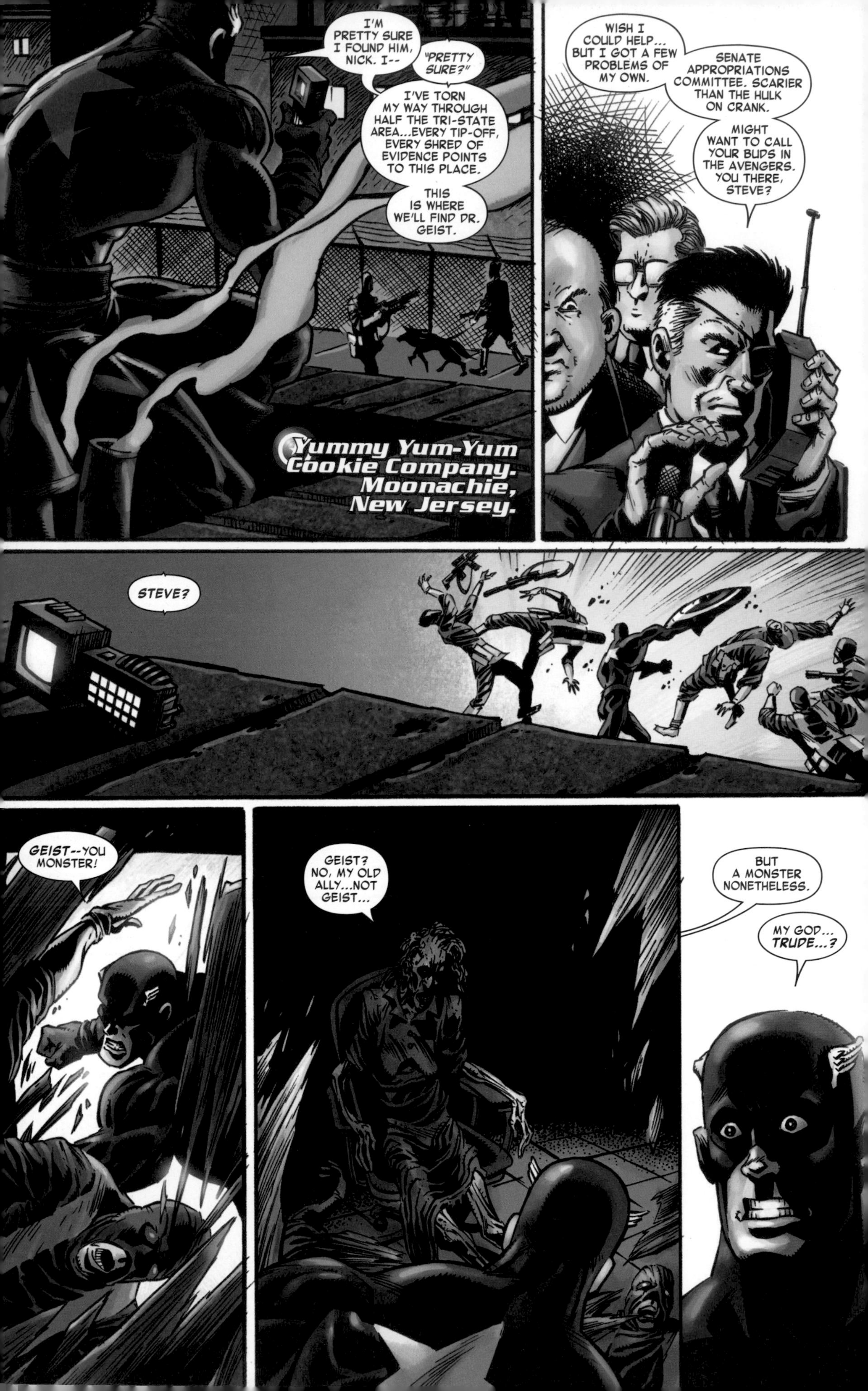
I'M PRETTY SURE I FOUND HIM, NICK. I--
"PRETTY SURE?"
I'VE TORN MY WAY THROUGH HALF THE TRI-STATE AREA...EVERY TIP-OFF, EVERY SHRED OF EVIDENCE POINTS TO THIS PLACE.
THIS IS WHERE WE'LL FIND DR. GEIST.
Yummy Yum-Yum Cookie Company. Moonachie, New Jersey.
WISH I COULD HELP... BUT I GOT A FEW PROBLEMS OF MY OWN.
SENATE APPROPRIATIONS COMMITTEE. SCARIER THAN THE HULK ON CRANK.
MIGHT WANT TO CALL YOUR BUDS IN THE AVENGERS. YOU THERE, STEVE?
STEVE?
GEIST--YOU MONSTER!
GEIST? NO, MY OLD ALLY...NOT GEIST...
BUT A MONSTER NONETHELESS.
MY GOD... TRUDE...?

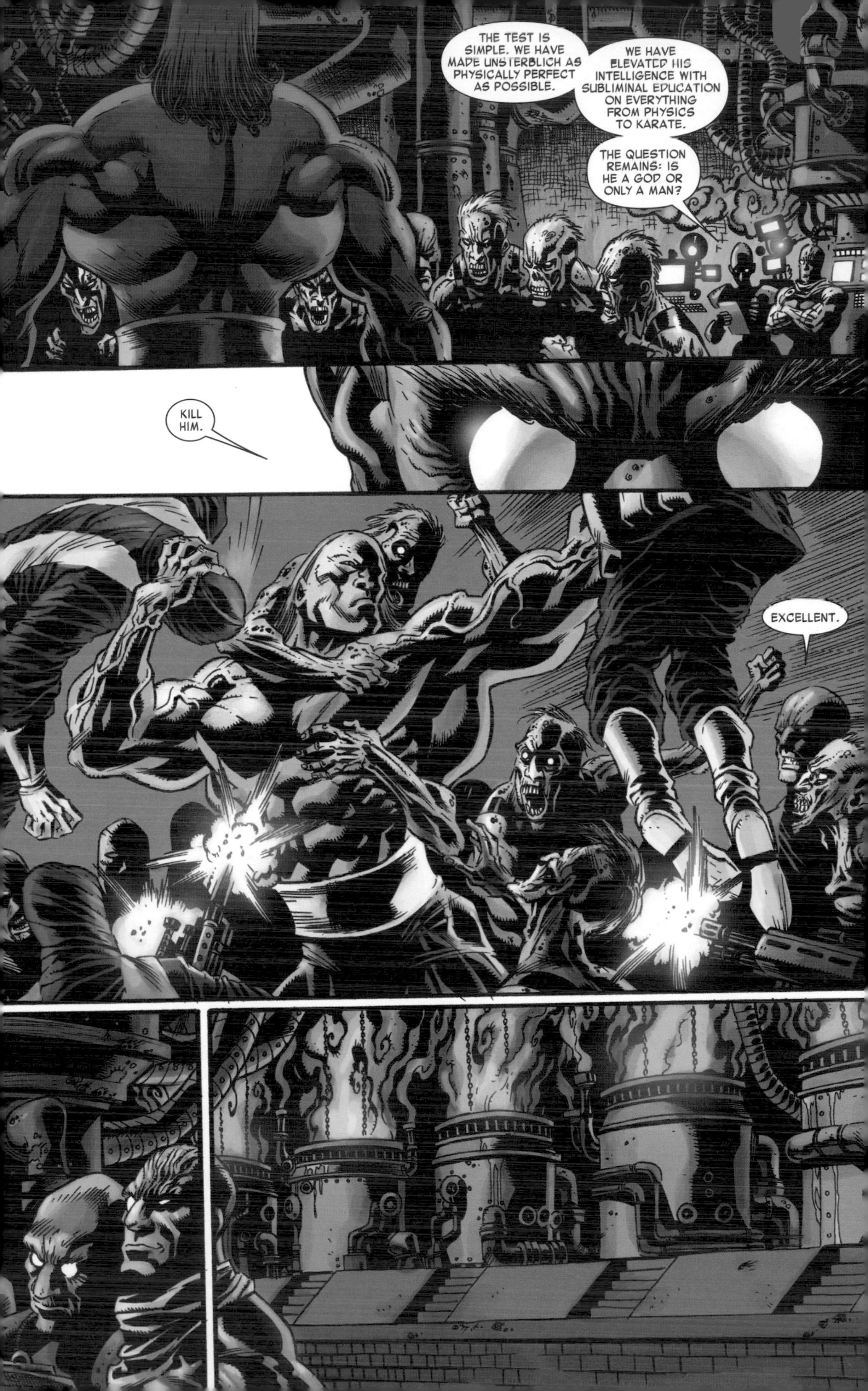
THE TEST IS SIMPLE. WE HAVE MADE UNSTERBLICH AS PHYSICALLY PERFECT AS POSSIBLE.
WE HAVE ELEVATED HIS INTELLIGENCE WITH SUBLIMINAL EDUCATION ON EVERYTHING FROM PHYSICS TO KARATE.
THE QUESTION REMAINS: IS HE A GOD OR ONLY A MAN?
KILL HIM.
EXCELLENT.

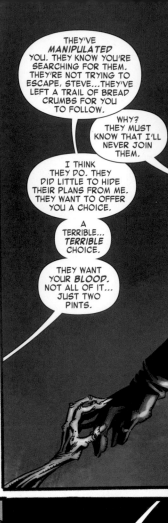

TRUDE! HOW DID THIS HAPPEN?

WH-WHAT HAVE THEY *DONE* TO YOU?

AFTER I...DIED... THEY TORE ME FROM MY GRAVE AND USED THEIR *BLACK SORCERY* TO *BRING ME BACK.*

THEY COULD HAVE BROUGHT ME ALL THE WAY BACK, BUT THEY THOUGHT THAT *THIS* WOULD MAKE A MORE ELOQUENT POINT.

WHAT... *POINT?*

THEY'VE *MANIPULATED* YOU. THEY KNOW YOU'RE SEARCHING FOR THEM. THEY'RE NOT TRYING TO ESCAPE, STEVE...THEY'VE LEFT A TRAIL OF BREAD CRUMBS FOR YOU TO FOLLOW.

WHY? THEY MUST KNOW THAT I'LL NEVER JOIN THEM.

I THINK THEY DO. THEY DID LITTLE TO HIDE THEIR PLANS FROM ME. THEY WANT TO OFFER YOU A CHOICE.

A TERRIBLE... *TERRIBLE* CHOICE.

THEY WANT YOUR *BLOOD.* NOT ALL OF IT... JUST TWO PINTS.

OH, CAPTAIN... OH MY DEAR STEVE...THEY ARE THE *CRUELEST* OF MONSTERS.

IT DOESN'T SURPRISE ME. THEY STOLE SOME BEFORE. MINE AND THOR'S.

I DON'T KNOW IF THEY'RE TRYING TO DUPLICATE THE SUPER-SOLDIER PROCESS OR USE MY BLOOD AS PART OF THEIR QUEST FOR IMMORTALITY...

BUT THEY HAVE TO KNOW THAT I'LL NEVER AGREE TO THAT.

THEY DO KNOW THAT. THAT'S WHY THEY RESURRECTED ME. SO YOU CAN SEE THE HELL THAT I'M IN. THEY WANT TO *HURT* YOU.

NOW...IMAGINE THAT HURT MAGNIFIED TEN THOUSAND TIMES. IMAGINE USING THAT EVIL SCIENCE TO INFLICT A *WOUND* ON THE ENTIRE AMERICAN PSYCHE. A WOUND THAT WOULD NEVER HEAL...

STEVE... IF YOU REFUSE TO GIVE THEM YOUR BLOOD...

...THEN HYDRA WILL USE THE LAZARUS FORMULA TO RAISE *ALL THE DEAD IN ARLINGTON CEMETERY.*

ALL OF YOUR HEROES, ALL OF AMERICA'S SACRED DEAD...RESURRECTED AS SHAMBLING, DECAYING MONSTERS.

THAT IS YOUR CHOICE...

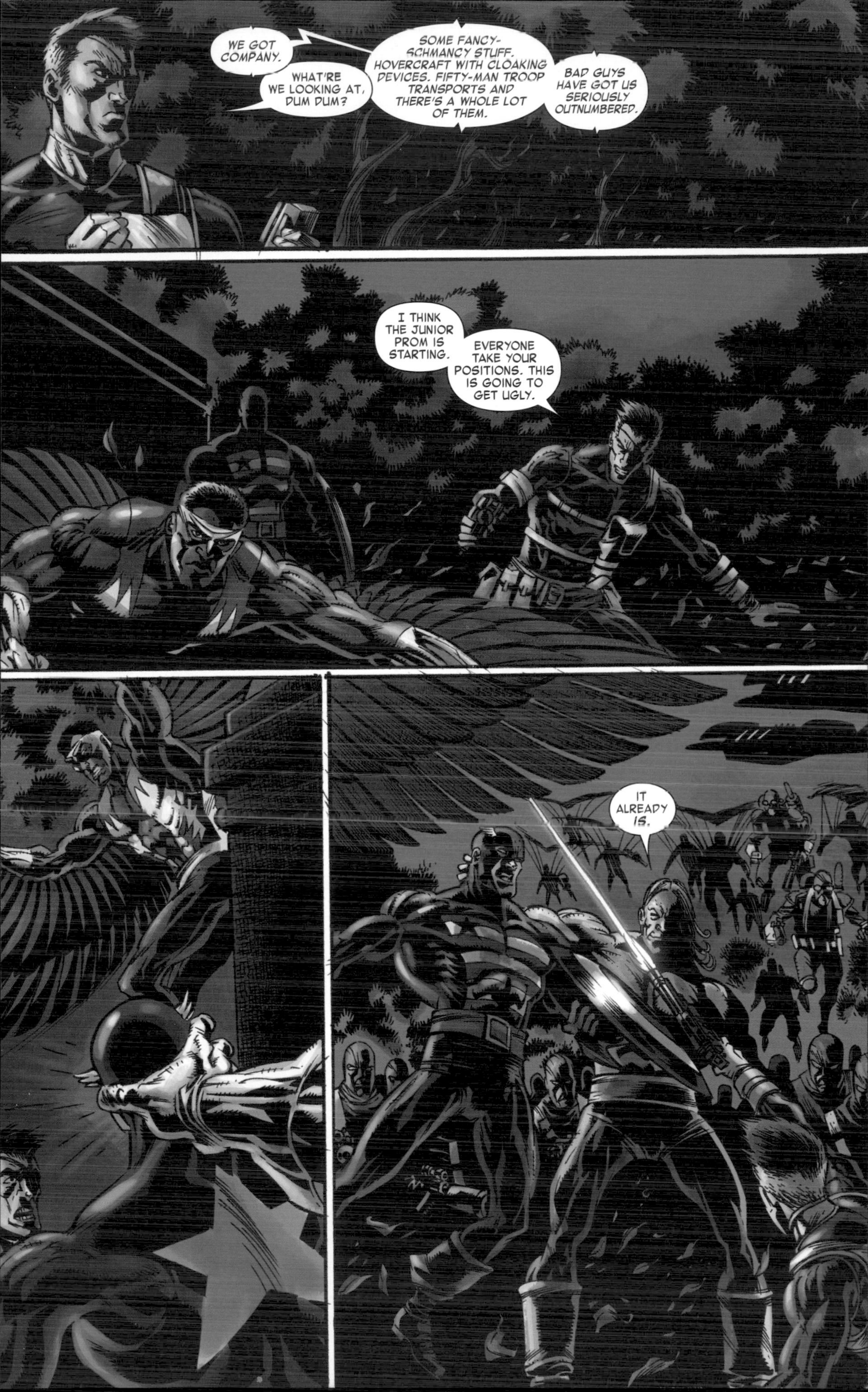
WE GOT COMPANY.
WHAT'RE WE LOOKING AT, DUM DUM?
SOME FANCY-SCHMANCY STUFF. HOVERCRAFT WITH CLOAKING DEVICES. FIFTY-MAN TROOP TRANSPORTS AND THERE'S A WHOLE LOT OF THEM.
BAD GUYS HAVE GOT US SERIOUSLY OUTNUMBERED.
I THINK THE JUNIOR PROM IS STARTING.
EVERYONE TAKE YOUR POSITIONS. THIS IS GOING TO GET UGLY.
IT ALREADY IS.

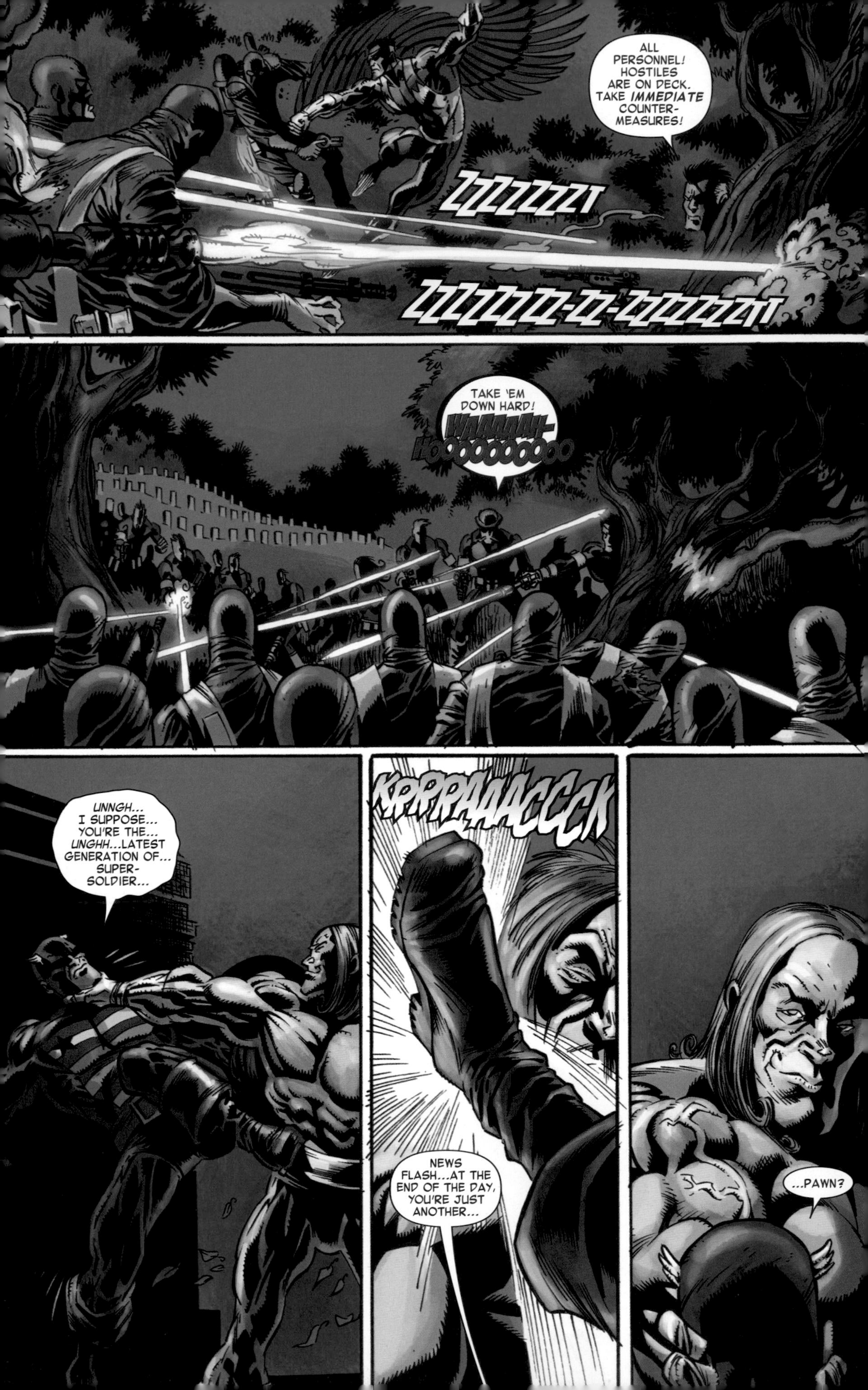
ALL PERSONNEL! HOSTILES ARE ON DECK. TAKE IMMEDIATE COUNTER-MEASURES!
ZZZZZZZT
ZZZZZZZZ-ZZ-ZZZZZZZZTT
TAKE 'EM DOWN HARD! WAAAAAH-HOOOOOOOOOOO
UNNGH... I SUPPOSE... YOU'RE THE... UNGHH...LATEST GENERATION OF... SUPER-SOLDIER...
KRRRAAACCCK
NEWS FLASH...AT THE END OF THE DAY, YOU'RE JUST ANOTHER...
...PAWN?

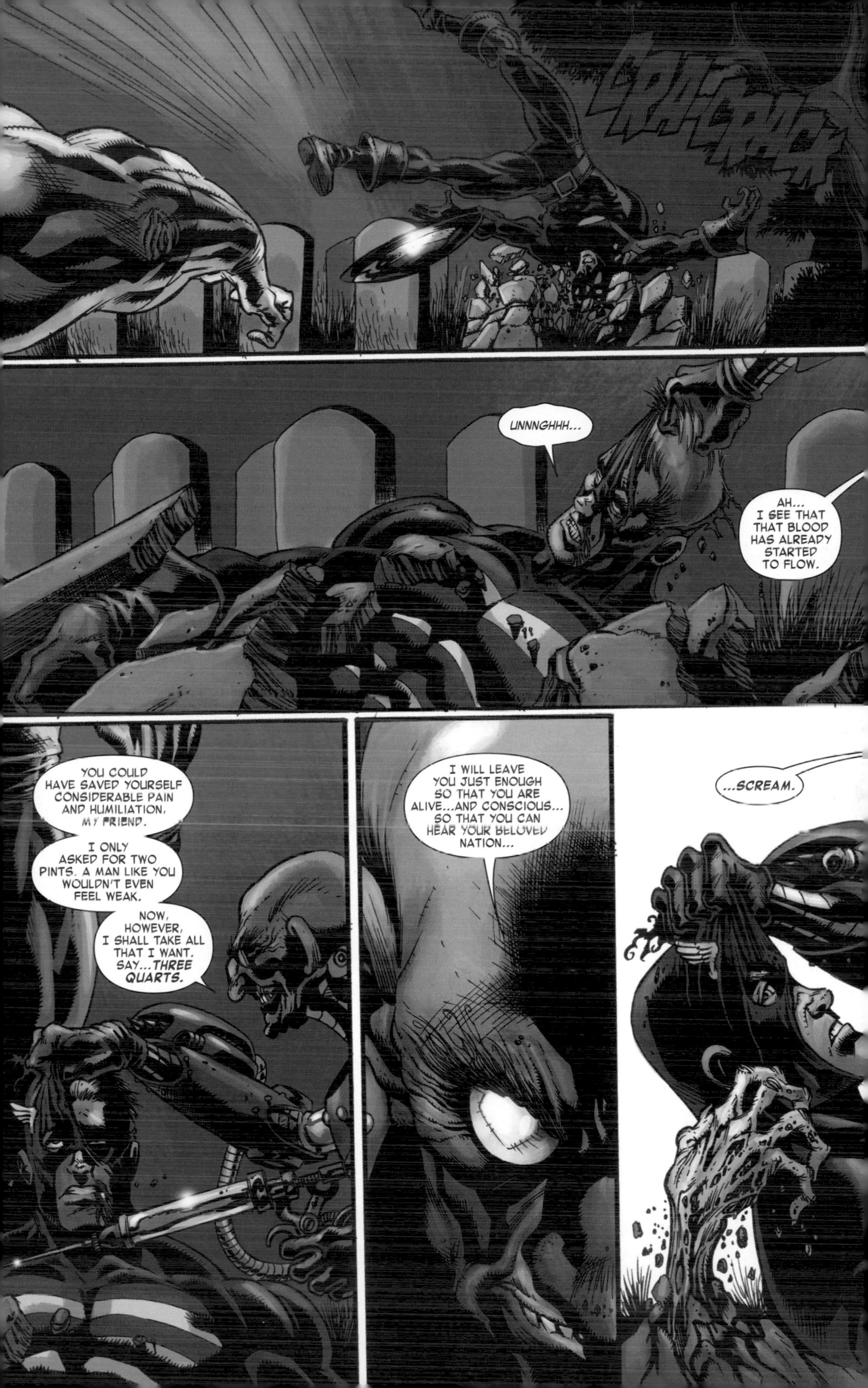
CRACKCRACK
UNNNGHHH...
AH... I SEE THAT THAT BLOOD HAS ALREADY STARTED TO FLOW.
YOU COULD HAVE SAVED YOURSELF CONSIDERABLE PAIN AND HUMILIATION, MY FRIEND.
I ONLY ASKED FOR TWO PINTS. A MAN LIKE YOU WOULDN'T EVEN FEEL WEAK.
NOW, HOWEVER, I SHALL TAKE ALL THAT I WANT. SAY...THREE QUARTS.
I WILL LEAVE YOU JUST ENOUGH SO THAT YOU ARE ALIVE...AND CONSCIOUS... SO THAT YOU CAN HEAR YOUR BELOVED NATION...
...SCREAM.

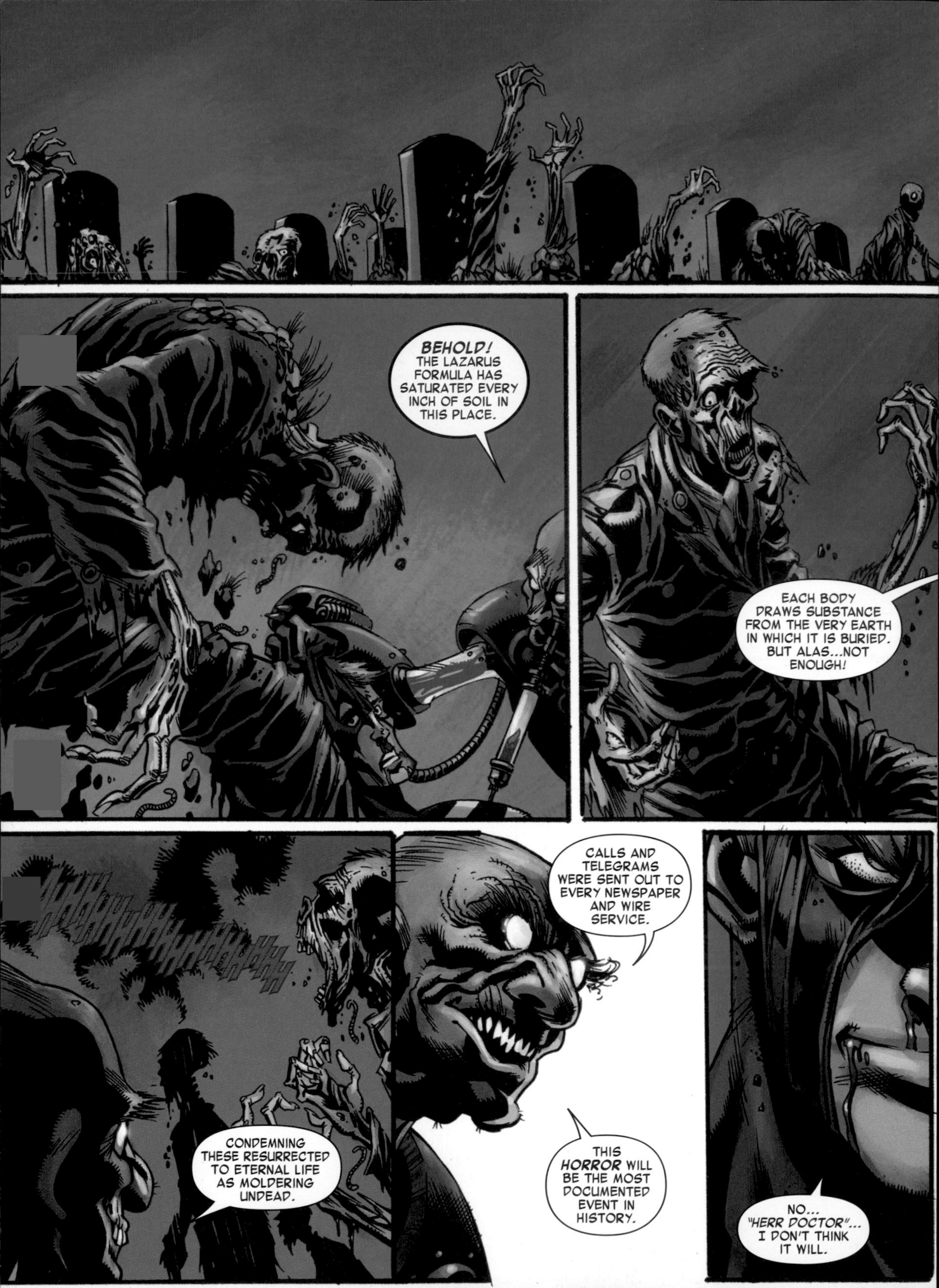
BEHOLD! THE LAZARUS FORMULA HAS SATURATED EVERY INCH OF SOIL IN THIS PLACE.
EACH BODY DRAWS SUBSTANCE FROM THE VERY EARTH IN WHICH IT IS BURIED. BUT ALAS...NOT ENOUGH!
CONDEMNING THESE RESURRECTED TO ETERNAL LIFE AS MOLDERING UNDEAD.
CALLS AND TELEGRAMS WERE SENT OUT TO EVERY NEWSPAPER AND WIRE SERVICE.
THIS HORROR WILL BE THE MOST DOCUMENTED EVENT IN HISTORY.
NO... "HERR DOCTOR"... I DON'T THINK IT WILL.

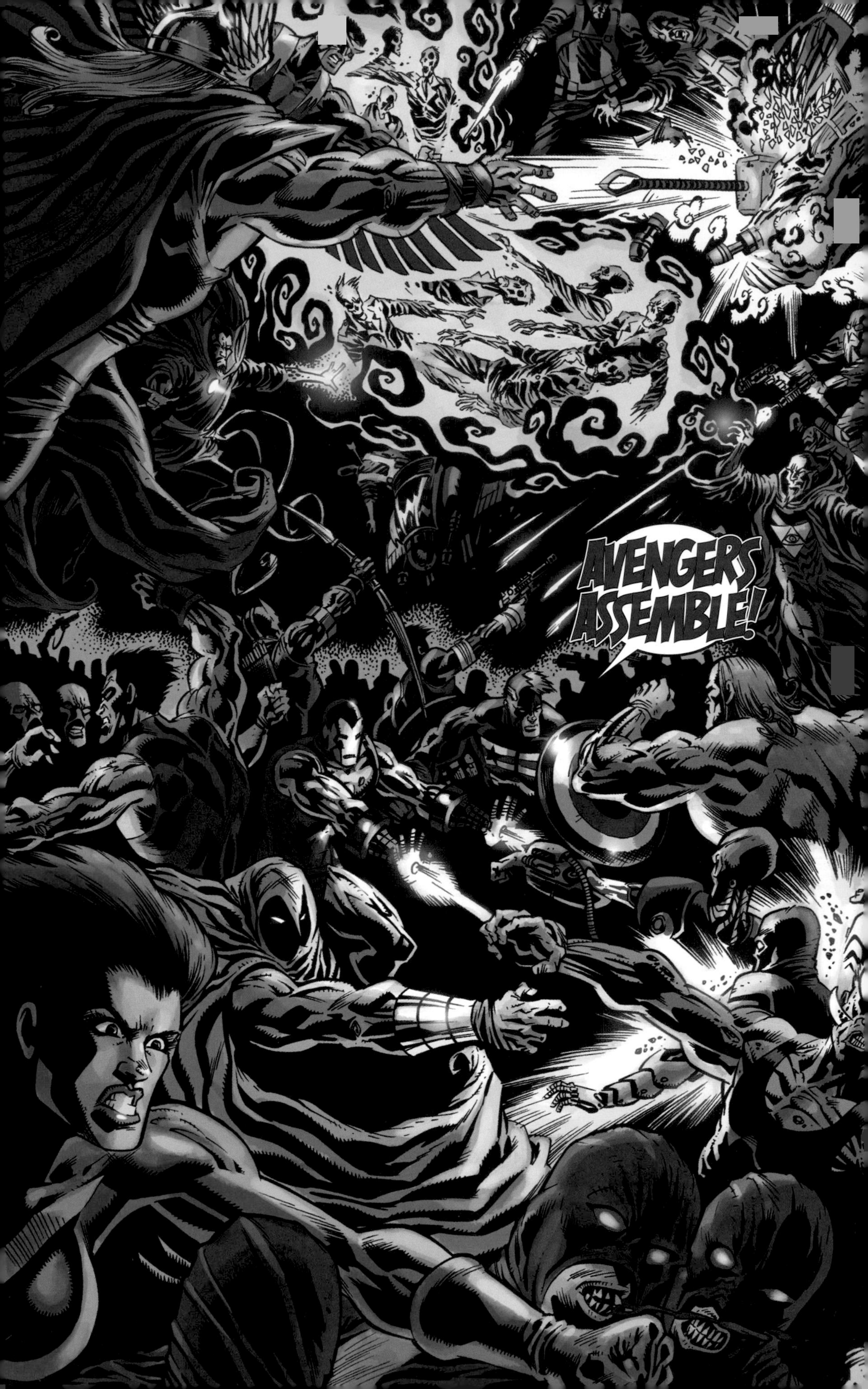
AVENGERS ASSEMBLE!

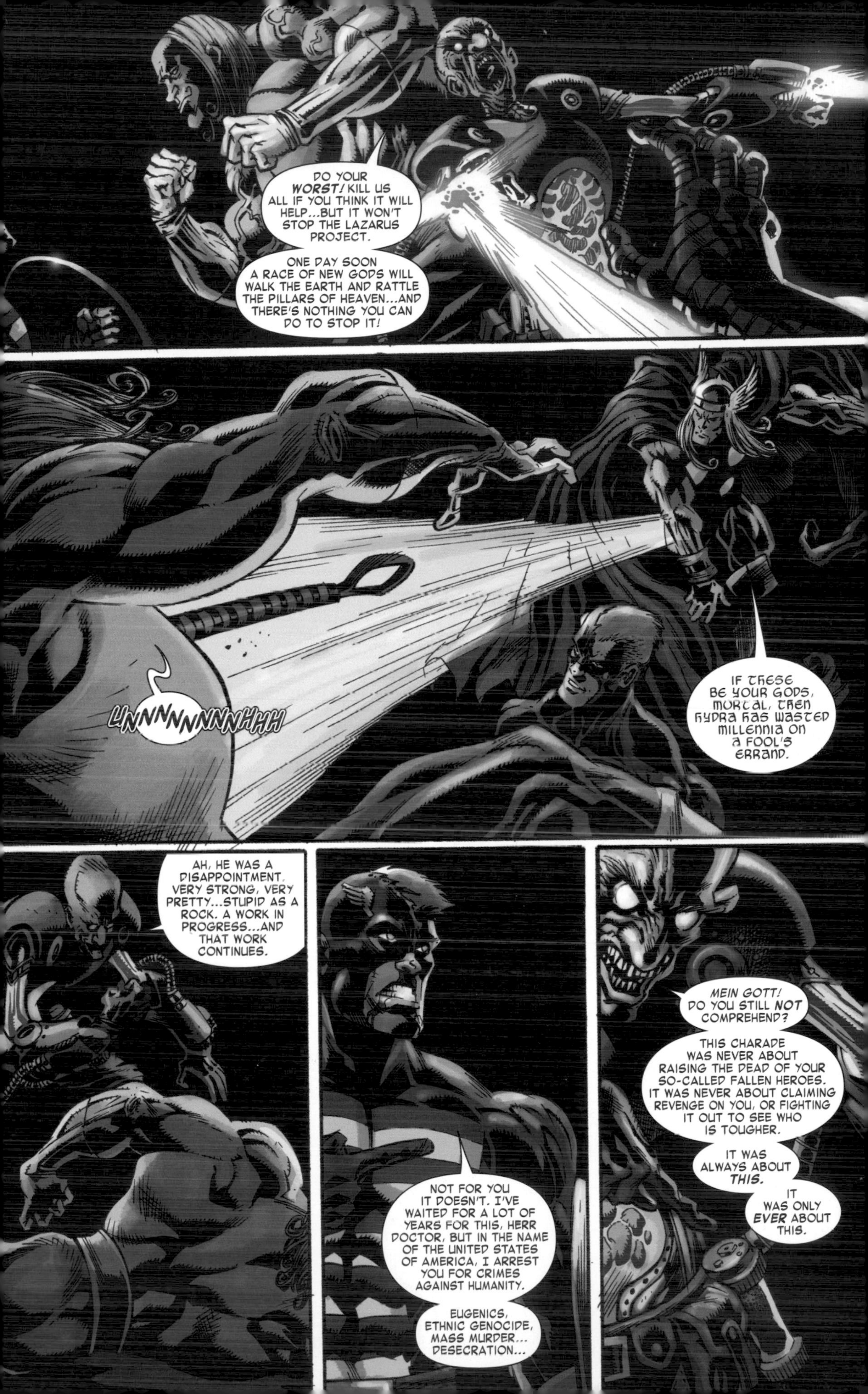

DO YOUR WORST! KILL US ALL IF YOU THINK IT WILL HELP...BUT IT WON'T STOP THE LAZARUS PROJECT.
ONE DAY SOON A RACE OF NEW GODS WILL WALK THE EARTH AND RATTLE THE PILLARS OF HEAVEN...AND THERE'S NOTHING YOU CAN DO TO STOP IT!
UNNNNNNNNHHH
IF THESE BE YOUR GODS, MORTAL, THEN HYDRA HAS WASTED MILLENNIA ON A FOOL'S ERRAND.
AH, HE WAS A DISAPPOINTMENT. VERY STRONG, VERY PRETTY...STUPID AS A ROCK. A WORK IN PROGRESS...AND THAT WORK CONTINUES.
NOT FOR YOU IT DOESN'T. I'VE WAITED FOR A LOT OF YEARS FOR THIS, HERR DOCTOR, BUT IN THE NAME OF THE UNITED STATES OF AMERICA, I ARREST YOU FOR CRIMES AGAINST HUMANITY.
EUGENICS, ETHNIC GENOCIDE, MASS MURDER... DESECRATION...
MEIN GOTT! DO YOU STILL NOT COMPREHEND?
THIS CHARADE WAS NEVER ABOUT RAISING THE DEAD OF YOUR SO-CALLED FALLEN HEROES. IT WAS NEVER ABOUT CLAIMING REVENGE ON YOU, OR FIGHTING IT OUT TO SEE WHO IS TOUGHER.
IT WAS ALWAYS ABOUT THIS.
IT WAS ONLY EVER ABOUT THIS.

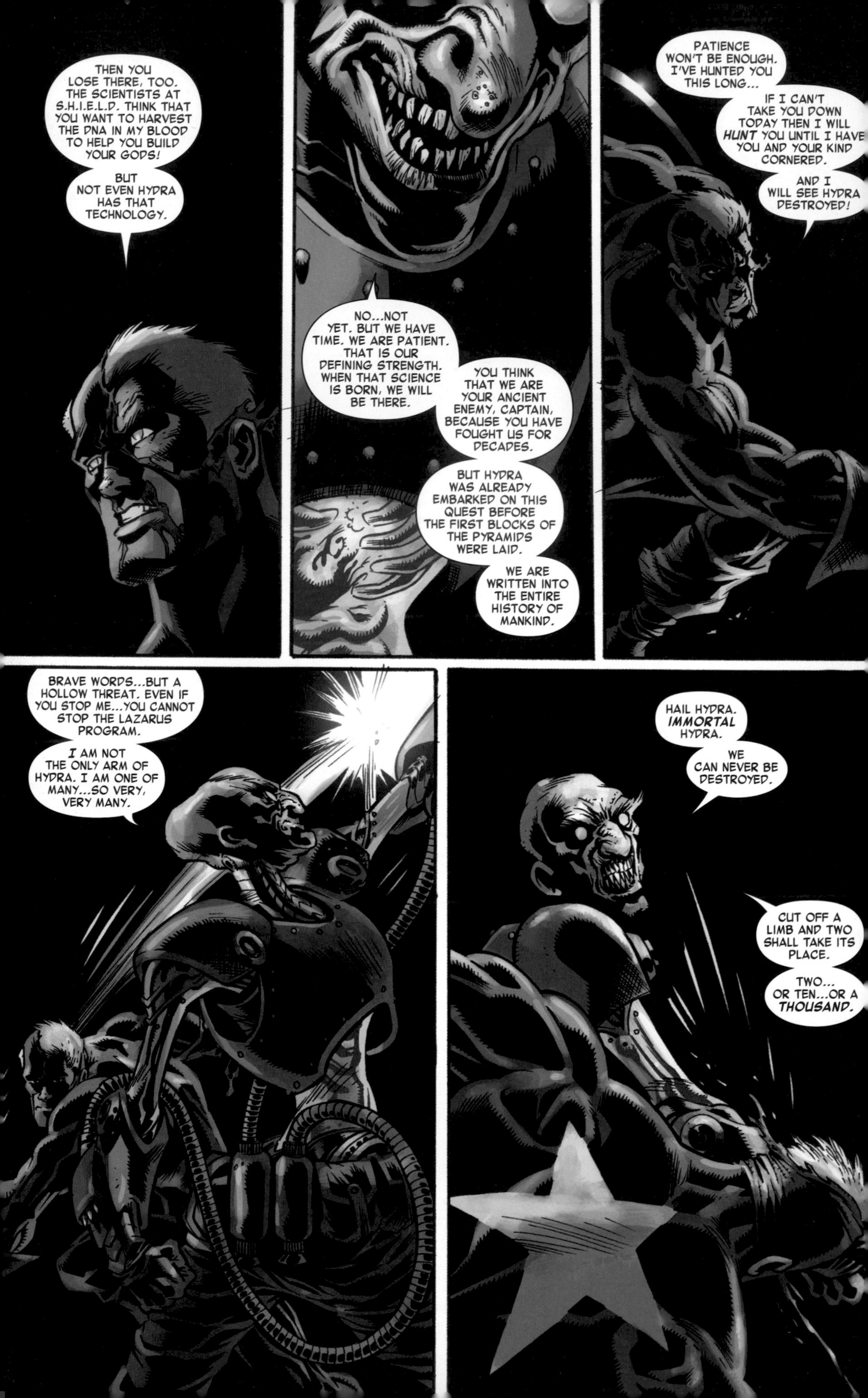
THEN YOU LOSE THERE, TOO. THE SCIENTISTS AT S.H.I.E.L.D. THINK THAT YOU WANT TO HARVEST THE DNA IN MY BLOOD TO HELP YOU BUILD YOUR GODS!
BUT NOT EVEN HYDRA HAS THAT TECHNOLOGY.
NO...NOT YET. BUT WE HAVE TIME. WE ARE PATIENT. THAT IS OUR DEFINING STRENGTH. WHEN THAT SCIENCE IS BORN, WE WILL BE THERE.
YOU THINK THAT WE ARE YOUR ANCIENT ENEMY, CAPTAIN, BECAUSE YOU HAVE FOUGHT US FOR DECADES.
BUT HYDRA WAS ALREADY EMBARKED ON THIS QUEST BEFORE THE FIRST BLOCKS OF THE PYRAMIDS WERE LAID.
WE ARE WRITTEN INTO THE ENTIRE HISTORY OF MANKIND.
PATIENCE WON'T BE ENOUGH. I'VE HUNTED YOU THIS LONG...
IF I CAN'T TAKE YOU DOWN TODAY THEN I WILL **HUNT** YOU UNTIL I HAVE YOU AND YOUR KIND CORNERED.
AND I WILL SEE HYDRA DESTROYED!
BRAVE WORDS...BUT A HOLLOW THREAT. EVEN IF YOU STOP ME...YOU CANNOT STOP THE LAZARUS PROGRAM.
I AM NOT THE ONLY ARM OF HYDRA. I AM ONE OF MANY...SO VERY, VERY MANY.
HAIL HYDRA. ***IMMORTAL*** HYDRA.
WE CAN NEVER BE DESTROYED.
CUT OFF A LIMB AND TWO SHALL TAKE ITS PLACE.
TWO... OR TEN...OR A ***THOUSAND.***

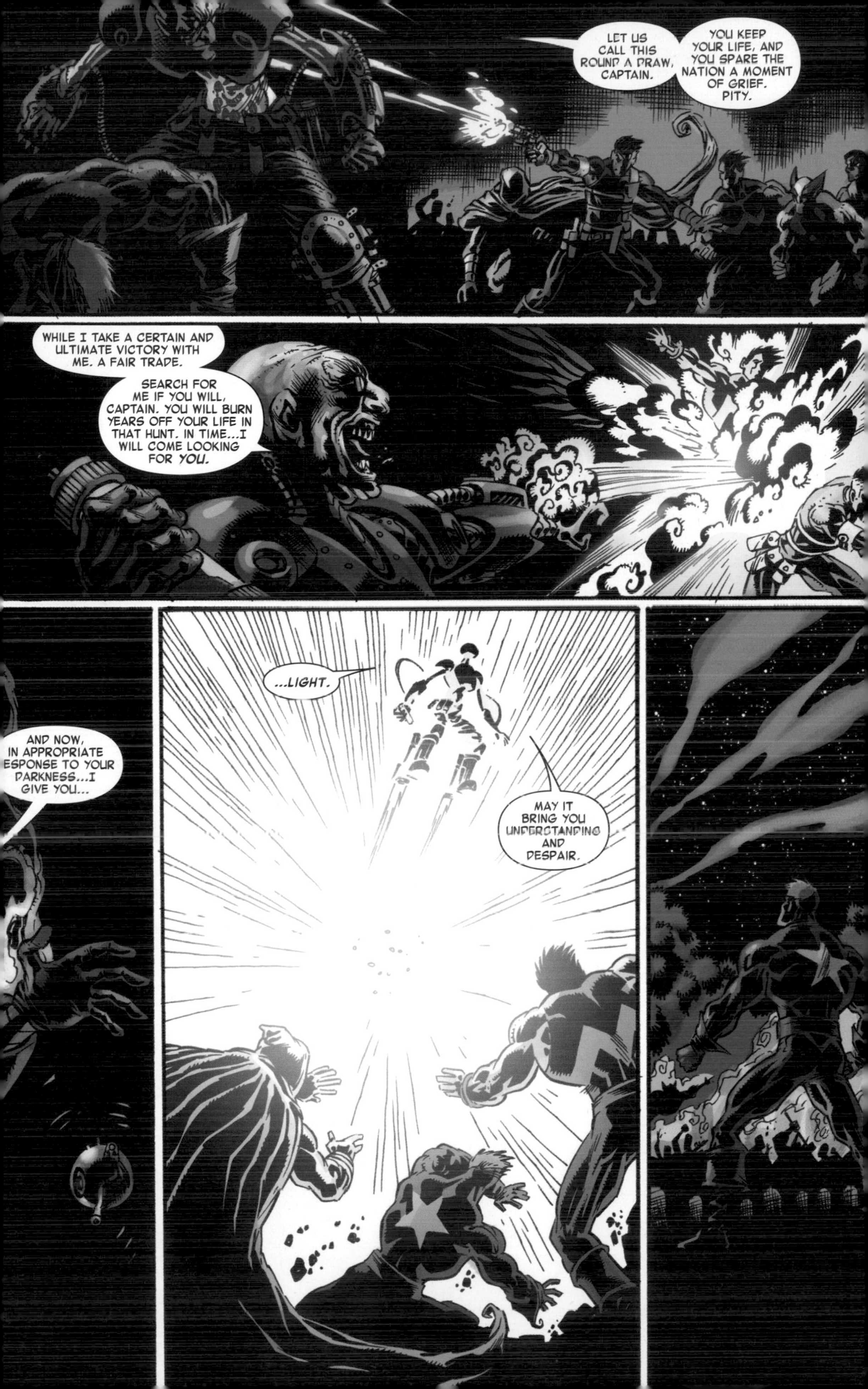
LET US CALL THIS ROUND A DRAW, CAPTAIN.
YOU KEEP YOUR LIFE, AND YOU SPARE THE NATION A MOMENT OF GRIEF. PITY.
WHILE I TAKE A CERTAIN AND ULTIMATE VICTORY WITH ME. A FAIR TRADE.
SEARCH FOR ME IF YOU WILL, CAPTAIN. YOU WILL BURN YEARS OFF YOUR LIFE IN THAT HUNT. IN TIME...I WILL COME LOOKING FOR *YOU.*
AND NOW, IN APPROPRIATE ESPONSE TO YOUR DARKNESS...I GIVE YOU...
...*LIGHT.*
MAY IT BRING YOU UNDERSTANDING AND DESPAIR.

MARVEL GRAPHIC NOVEL CAPTAIN AMERICA: HAIL HYDRA #5

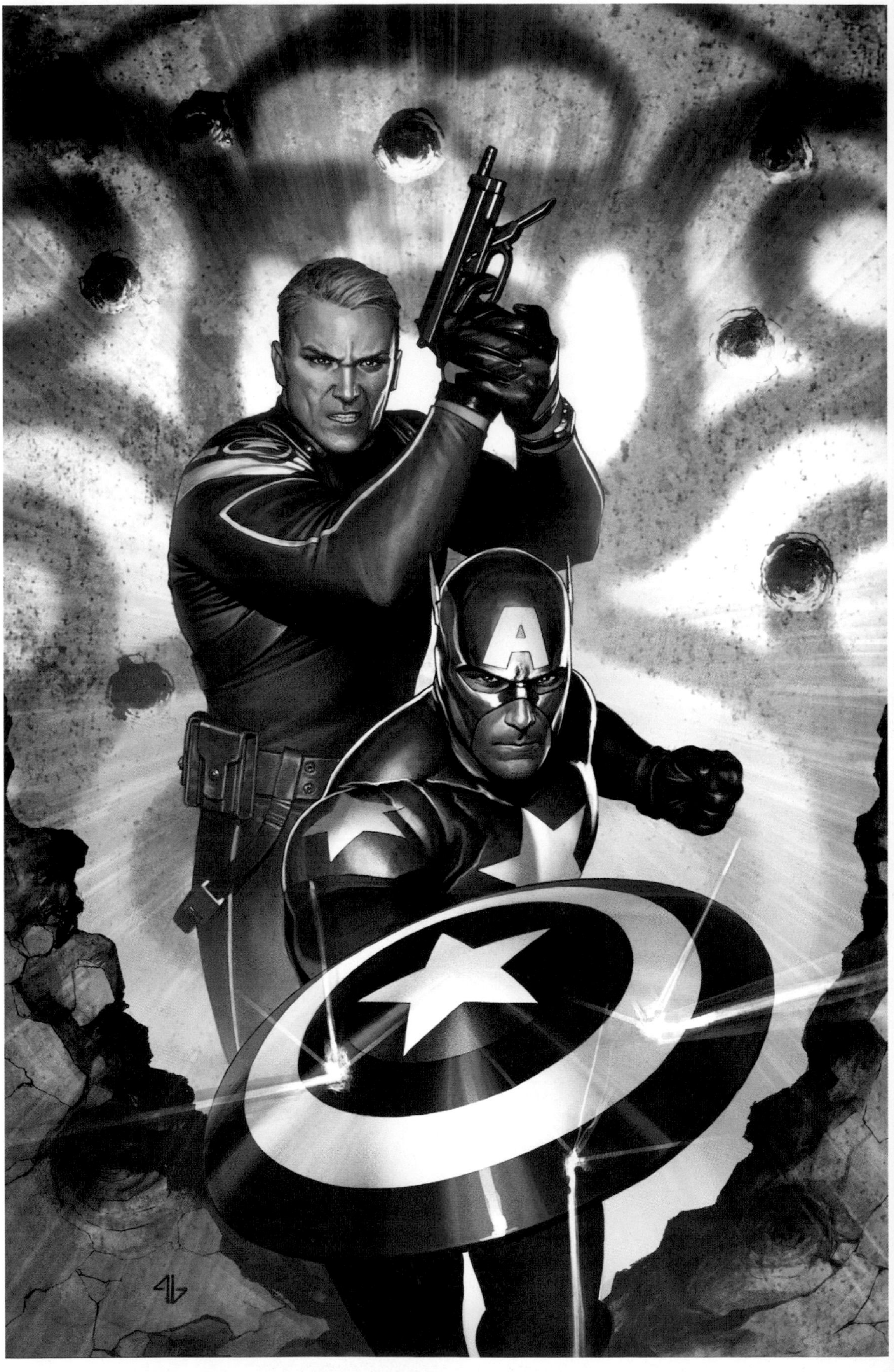

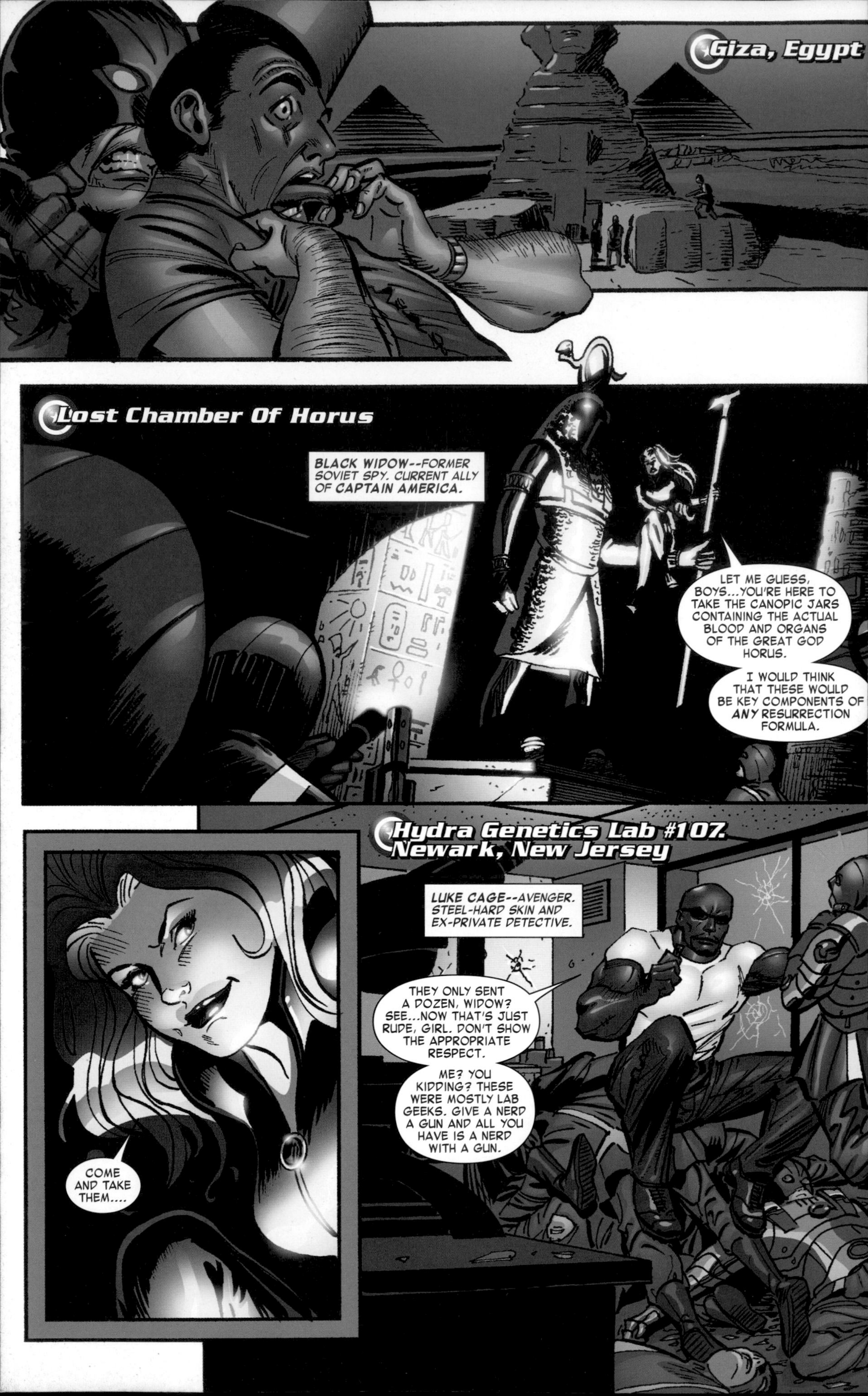
Giza, Egypt
Lost Chamber Of Horus
BLACK WIDOW--FORMER SOVIET SPY. CURRENT ALLY OF CAPTAIN AMERICA.
LET ME GUESS, BOYS...YOU'RE HERE TO TAKE THE CANOPIC JARS CONTAINING THE ACTUAL BLOOD AND ORGANS OF THE GREAT GOD HORUS.
I WOULD THINK THAT THESE WOULD BE KEY COMPONENTS OF ANY RESURRECTION FORMULA.
COME AND TAKE THEM....
Hydra Genetics Lab #107. Newark, New Jersey
LUKE CAGE--AVENGER. STEEL-HARD SKIN AND EX-PRIVATE DETECTIVE.
THEY ONLY SENT A DOZEN, WIDOW? SEE...NOW THAT'S JUST RUDE, GIRL. DON'T SHOW THE APPROPRIATE RESPECT.
ME? YOU KIDDING? THESE WERE MOSTLY LAB GEEKS. GIVE A NERD A GUN AND ALL YOU HAVE IS A NERD WITH A GUN.

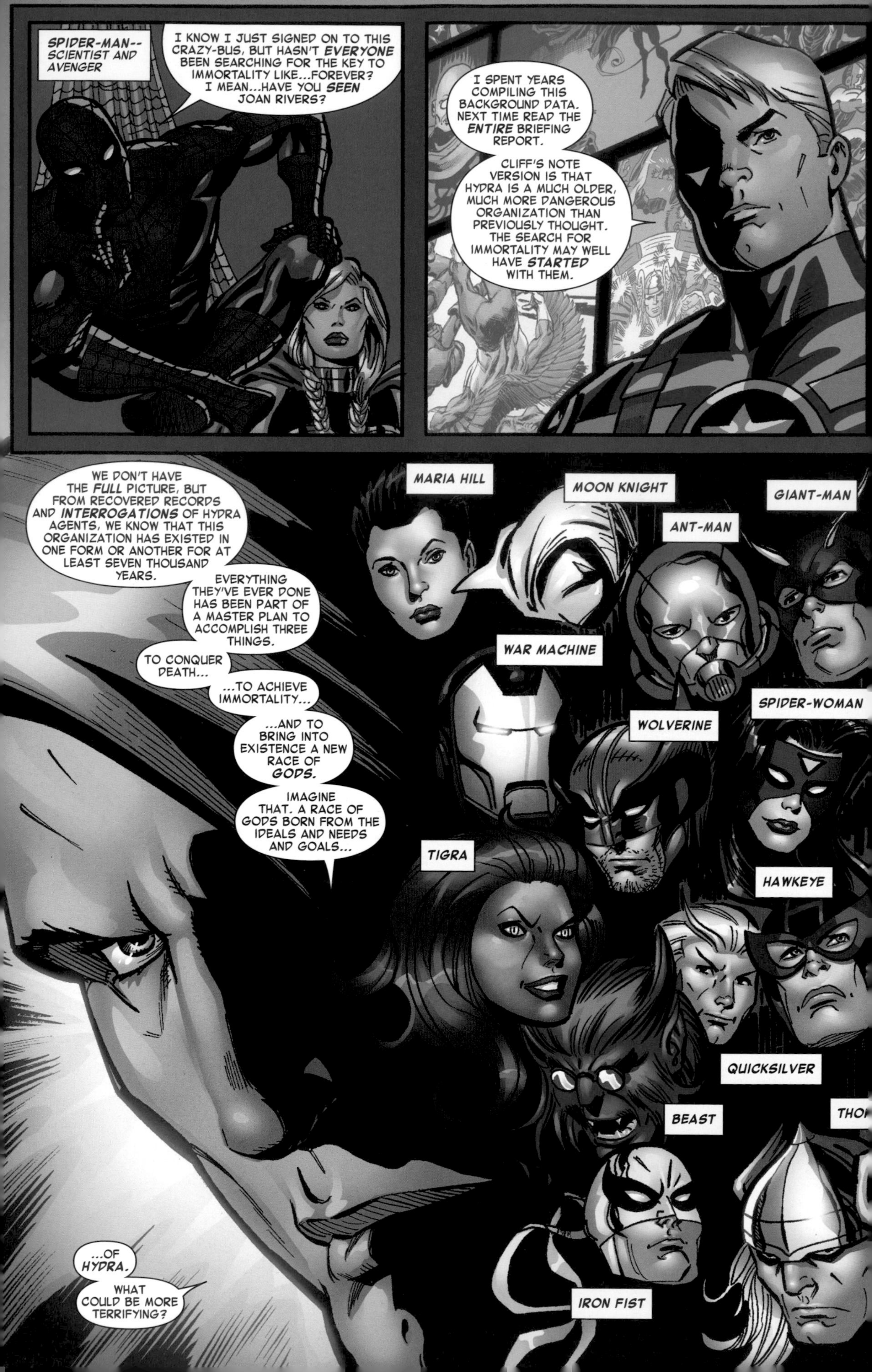
SPIDER-MAN-- SCIENTIST AND AVENGER
I KNOW I JUST SIGNED ON TO THIS CRAZY-BUS, BUT HASN'T EVERYONE BEEN SEARCHING FOR THE KEY TO IMMORTALITY LIKE...FOREVER? I MEAN...HAVE YOU SEEN JOAN RIVERS?
I SPENT YEARS COMPILING THIS BACKGROUND DATA. NEXT TIME READ THE ENTIRE BRIEFING REPORT.
CLIFF'S NOTE VERSION IS THAT HYDRA IS A MUCH OLDER, MUCH MORE DANGEROUS ORGANIZATION THAN PREVIOUSLY THOUGHT. THE SEARCH FOR IMMORTALITY MAY WELL HAVE STARTED WITH THEM.
WE DON'T HAVE THE FULL PICTURE, BUT FROM RECOVERED RECORDS AND INTERROGATIONS OF HYDRA AGENTS, WE KNOW THAT THIS ORGANIZATION HAS EXISTED IN ONE FORM OR ANOTHER FOR AT LEAST SEVEN THOUSAND YEARS.
EVERYTHING THEY'VE EVER DONE HAS BEEN PART OF A MASTER PLAN TO ACCOMPLISH THREE THINGS.
TO CONQUER DEATH...
...TO ACHIEVE IMMORTALITY...
...AND TO BRING INTO EXISTENCE A NEW RACE OF GODS.
IMAGINE THAT. A RACE OF GODS BORN FROM THE IDEALS AND NEEDS AND GOALS...
...OF HYDRA.
WHAT COULD BE MORE TERRIFYING?
MARIA HILL
MOON KNIGHT
GIANT-MAN
ANT-MAN
WAR MACHINE
SPIDER-WOMAN
WOLVERINE
TIGRA
HAWKEYE
QUICKSILVER
BEAST
IRON FIST

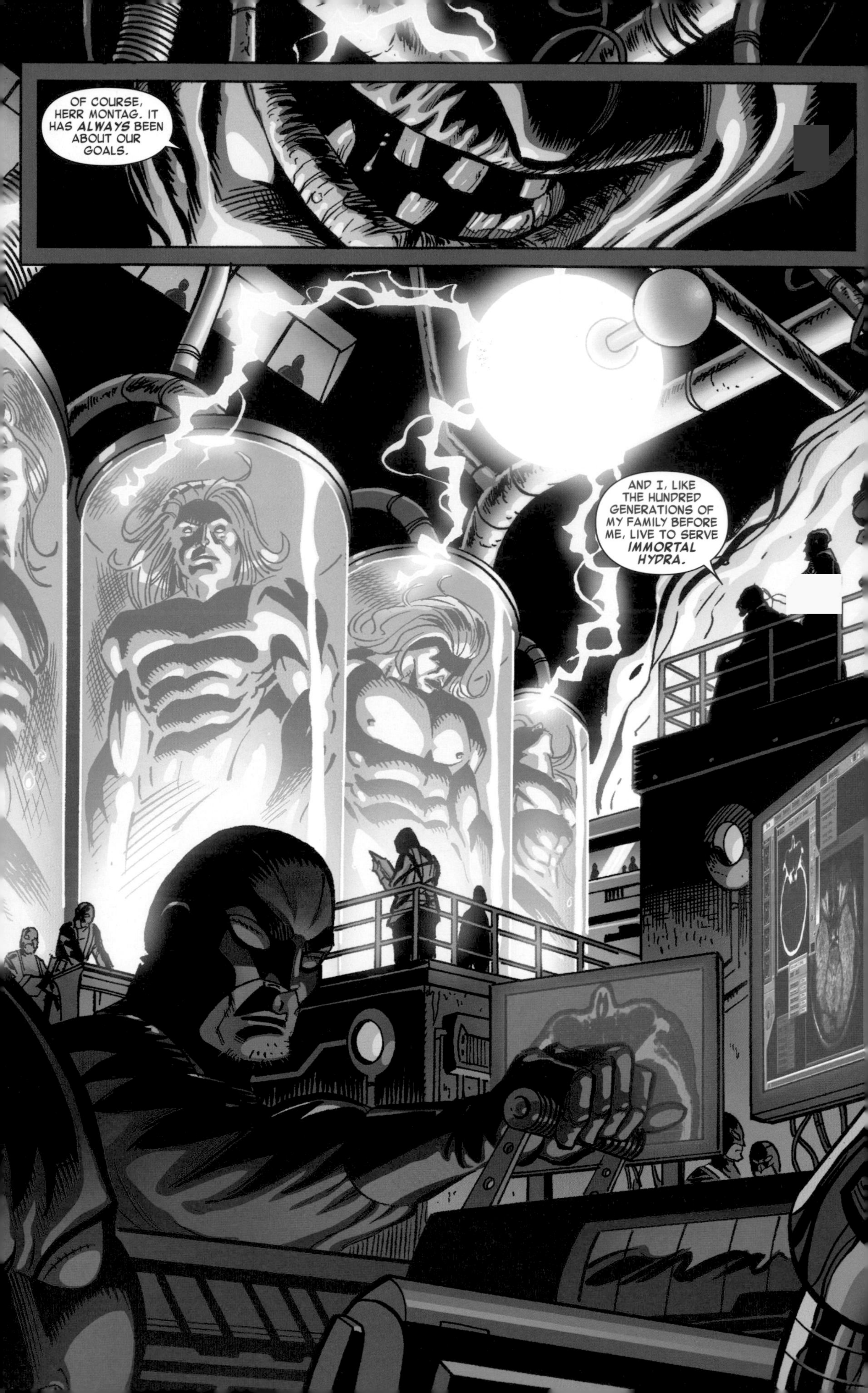
OF COURSE, HERR MONTAG. IT HAS ALWAYS BEEN ABOUT OUR GOALS.
AND I, LIKE THE HUNDRED GENERATIONS OF MY FAMILY BEFORE ME, LIVE TO SERVE IMMORTAL HYDRA.

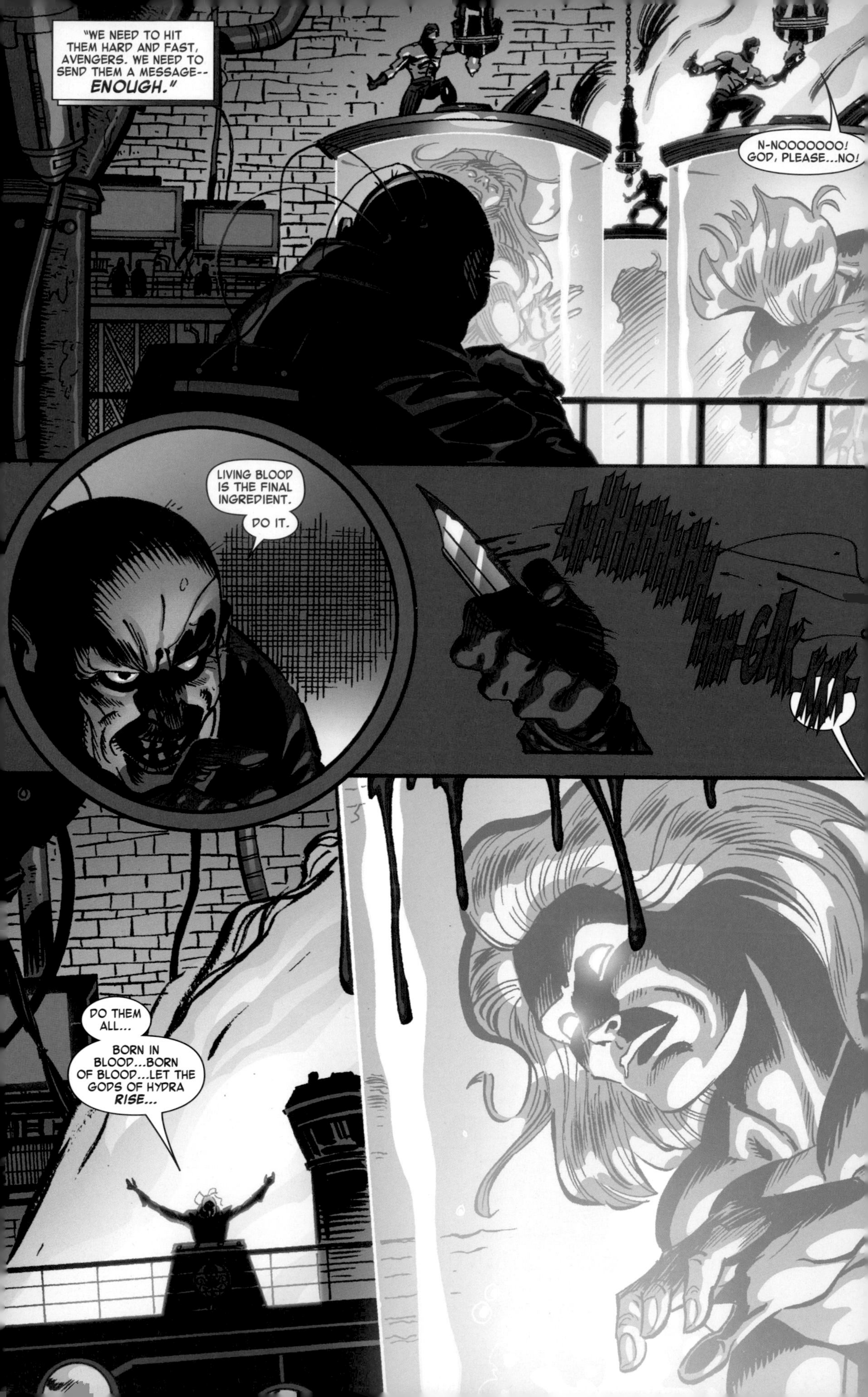
"WE NEED TO HIT THEM HARD AND FAST, AVENGERS. WE NEED TO SEND THEM A MESSAGE-- ENOUGH."
N-NOOOOOOO! GOD, PLEASE...NO!
LIVING BLOOD IS THE FINAL INGREDIENT.
DO IT.
DO THEM ALL...
BORN IN BLOOD...BORN OF BLOOD...LET THE GODS OF HYDRA RISE...

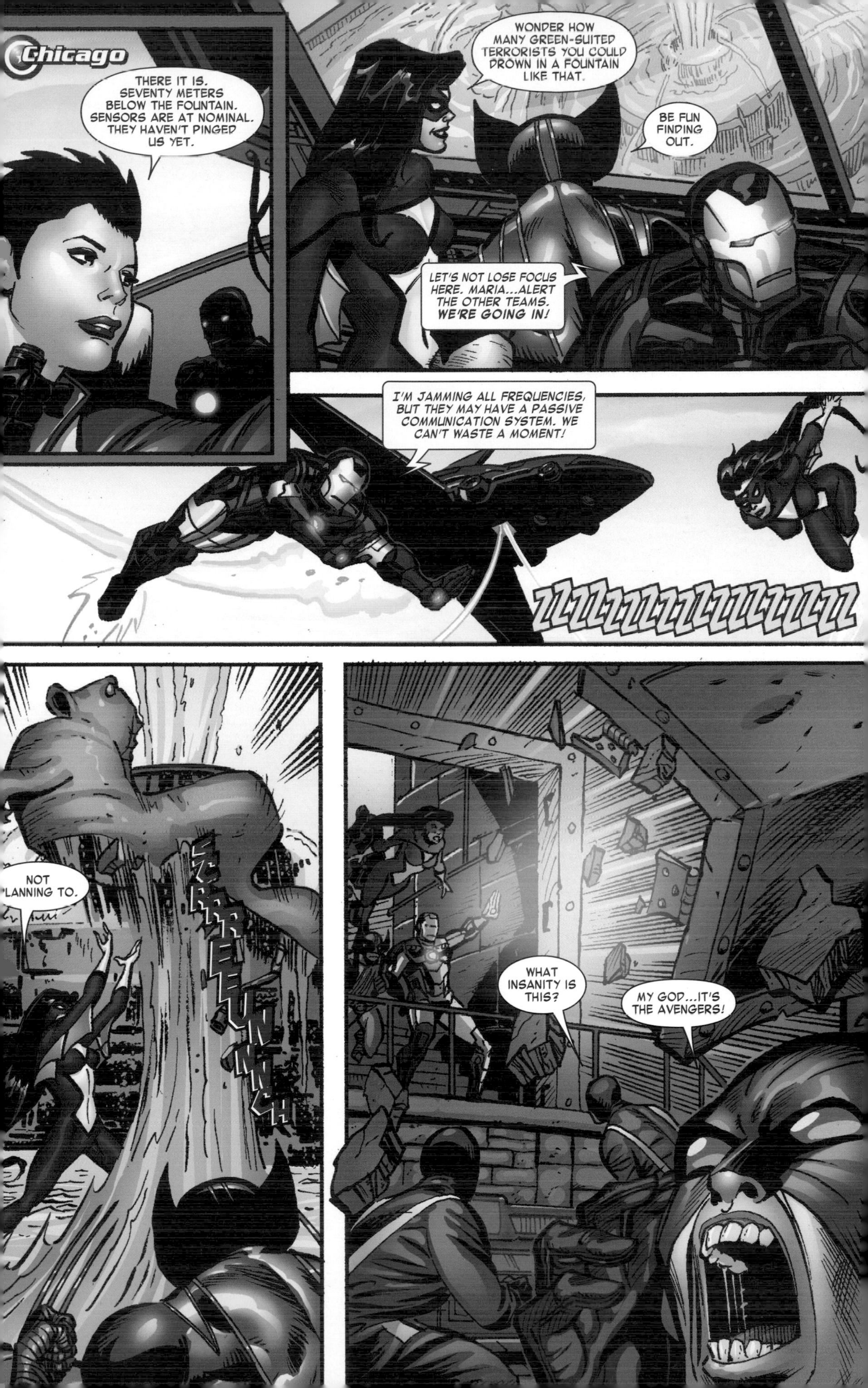
Chicago
THERE IT IS. SEVENTY METERS BELOW THE FOUNTAIN. SENSORS ARE AT NOMINAL. THEY HAVEN'T PINGED US YET.
WONDER HOW MANY GREEN-SUITED TERRORISTS YOU COULD DROWN IN A FOUNTAIN LIKE THAT.
BE FUN FINDING OUT.
LET'S NOT LOSE FOCUS HERE. MARIA...ALERT THE OTHER TEAMS. WE'RE GOING IN!
I'M JAMMING ALL FREQUENCIES, BUT THEY MAY HAVE A PASSIVE COMMUNICATION SYSTEM. WE CAN'T WASTE A MOMENT!
ZZZZZZZZZZZZZZZZZZZZ
NOT LANNING TO.
SKRREEUNNCH
WHAT INSANITY IS THIS?
MY GOD...IT'S THE AVENGERS!

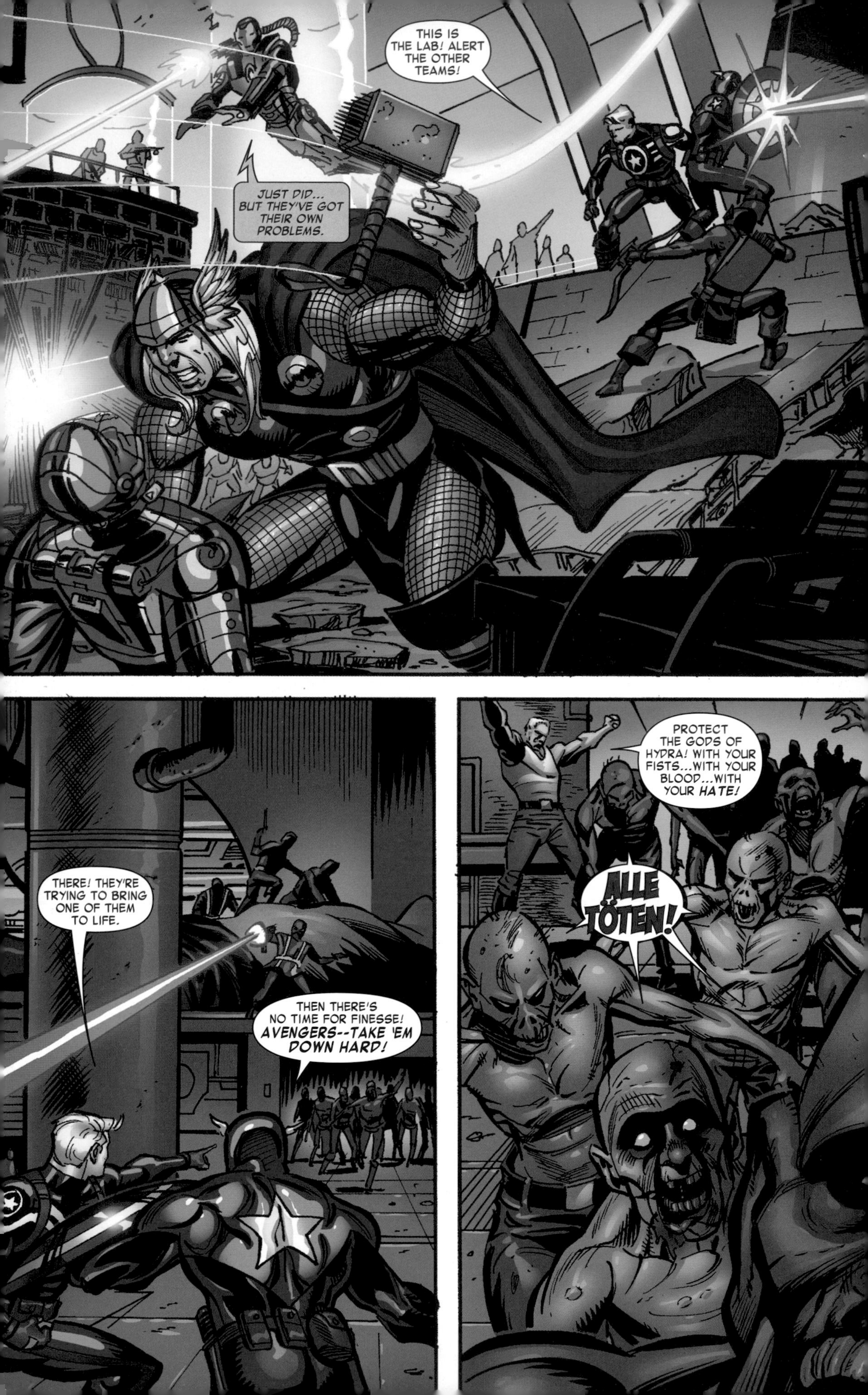
THIS IS THE LAB! ALERT THE OTHER TEAMS!
JUST DID... BUT THEY'VE GOT THEIR OWN PROBLEMS.
THERE! THEY'RE TRYING TO BRING ONE OF THEM TO LIFE.
THEN THERE'S NO TIME FOR FINESSE! AVENGERS--TAKE 'EM DOWN HARD!
PROTECT THE GODS OF HYDRA! WITH YOUR FISTS...WITH YOUR BLOOD...WITH YOUR HATE!
ALLE TÖTEN!

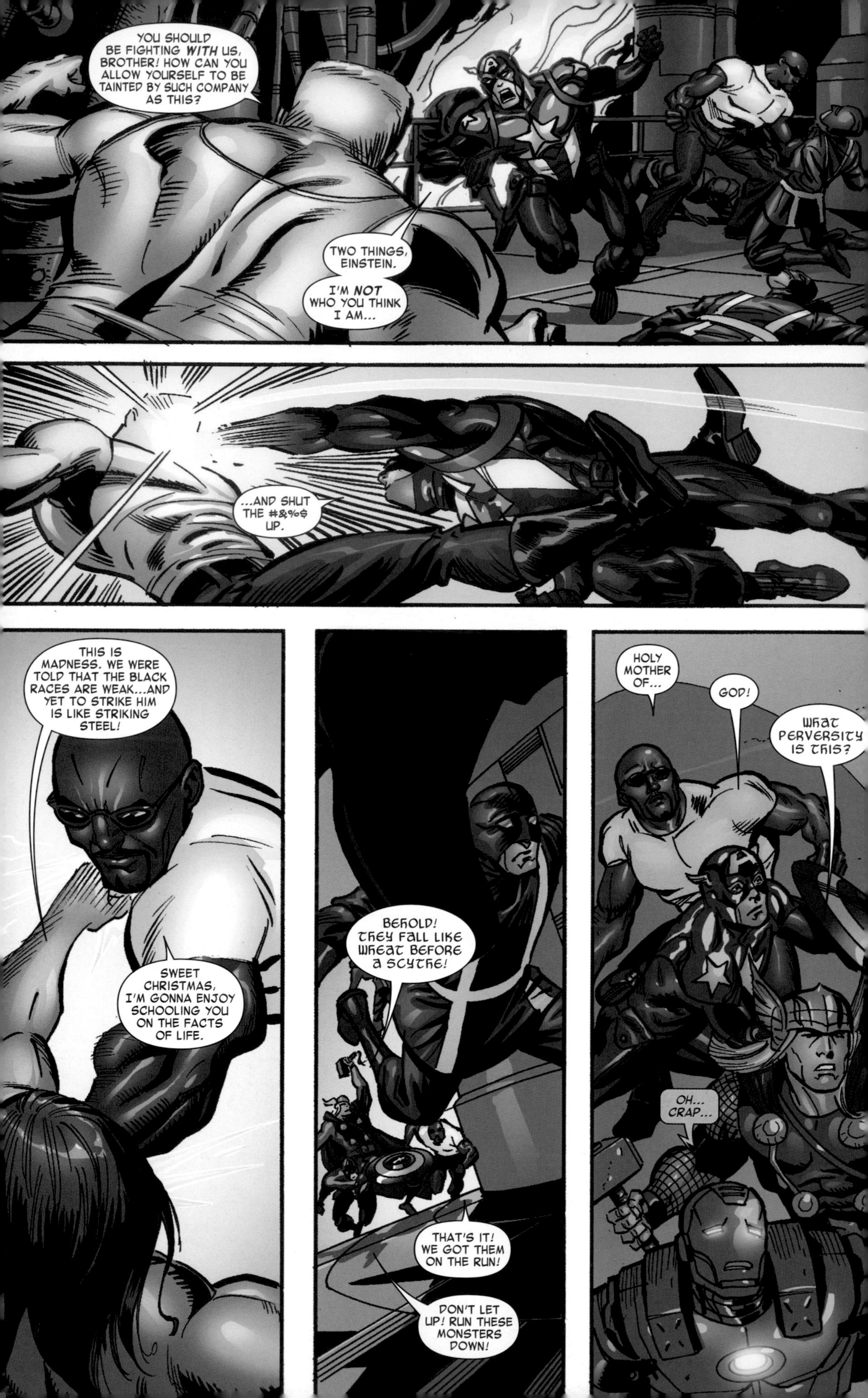

YOU SHOULD BE FIGHTING WITH US, BROTHER! HOW CAN YOU ALLOW YOURSELF TO BE TAINTED BY SUCH COMPANY AS THIS?
TWO THINGS, EINSTEIN.
I'M NOT WHO YOU THINK I AM...
...AND SHUT THE #&%$ UP.
THIS IS MADNESS. WE WERE TOLD THAT THE BLACK RACES ARE WEAK...AND YET TO STRIKE HIM IS LIKE STRIKING STEEL!
SWEET CHRISTMAS, I'M GONNA ENJOY SCHOOLING YOU ON THE FACTS OF LIFE.
BEHOLD! THEY FALL LIKE WHEAT BEFORE A SCYTHE!
THAT'S IT! WE GOT THEM ON THE RUN!
DON'T LET UP! RUN THESE MONSTERS DOWN!
HOLY MOTHER OF...
GOD!
WHAT PERVERSITY IS THIS?
OH... CRAP...

AND NOW...STEVE ROGERS... THE CAPTAIN AMERICA THAT *WAS*...THE HERO WHO WILL *NEVER* BE AGAIN...

I...

I CALL ON MY GOD TO PROVE TO YOU...TO ALL OF YOU...THAT THIS IS THE HOUR OF HYDRA. ALL GAMES ARE DONE, ALL RACES WON. ALL BATTLES ENDED.

...ahmmm... G-G-G...

IN THE NAME OF HOLY HYDRA. IN *THY NAME*, MY LORD...CRUSH THIS MAN AND BAPTIZE YOUR OWN IMMORTAL FLESH WITH BLOOD.

...GOD.

no.

W-WHAT? EXCUSE ME, LORD HYDRA... BUT I DID NOT...

no!

I AM GOD.

I AM.

I.

I.

NOT *WE*.

NOOOOO-- AIIIIIIIIEEEE! WHAT ARE YOU *DOING*?

I... SEE.

I...KNOW. I UNDERSTAND. I *am*.

MY MIND HAS COME FROM DARKNESS AND IS FILLED WITH LIGHT. WITH *ALL* LIGHT.

I SEE FORWARD AND BACKWARD. INTO ETERNITY. I SEE EVERYTHING. AS I WAS MEANT TO SEE EVERYTHING. AS I SHOULD SEE EVERYTHING.

I AM *EVERYTHING*.

YOU HAVE ACCOMPLISHED WONDERS. FLAWED MAN HAS MADE A *PERFECT* GOD.

PLEASE... I CANNOT LIVE OUTSIDE OF YOUR FLESH...

MAN IS MORTAL. ONLY GODS ARE MEANT TO LIVE FOREVER. HOW DO YOU, OF ALL PEOPLE, NOT KNOW THIS?

I *MADE* YOU...HAVE MERCY ON ME...

I AM ALL THINGS. I AM MERCY.

I AM A GOD...AS SUCH I BEND TO NO MORTAL WILL.

AND SO...

HYDRA WAS THE INSTRUMENT OF MY BIRTH...BUT THEY DO NOT OWN ME. MEN DO NOT OWN THE GODS.

I WILL NOT BEGIN THE FIRST HOUR OF MY OWN ETERNAL WANDERING BY ATTEMPTING TO DESTRO[Y] THAT WHICH FATE ITSELF HAS FASHIONED.

YOU HAVE WON THIS WAR, STEVE ROGERS.

CELEBRATE THAT VICTORY UNTIL THE NEXT WAR CALLS YOU.

I BLESS YOU AND BID YOU FAREWELL.

ONCE AND FUTURE CAPTAIN AMERICA.

HYDRA ISN'T DEAD, YOU KNOW... EVEN NOW. THEY WILL RISE AGAIN. IN SOME WAY, IN SOME FORM...

YEAH. IF WE'VE LEARNED ANYTHING ABOUT THE UNIVERSE, STEVE, IT'S THAT EVIL ENDURES.

BUT, AT THE RISK OF SOUNDING LIKE A BORN-AGAIN IDEALIST... I HAVE TO BELIEVE THAT SOMEONE WILL ALWAYS RISE TO OPPOSE IT. YOUR WHOLE LIFE IS PROOF OF THAT. MAYBE MINE, TOO.

SO... WHEN HYDRA RISES AGAIN... YOU...WE...WILL BE THERE TO FACE THEM.

The End

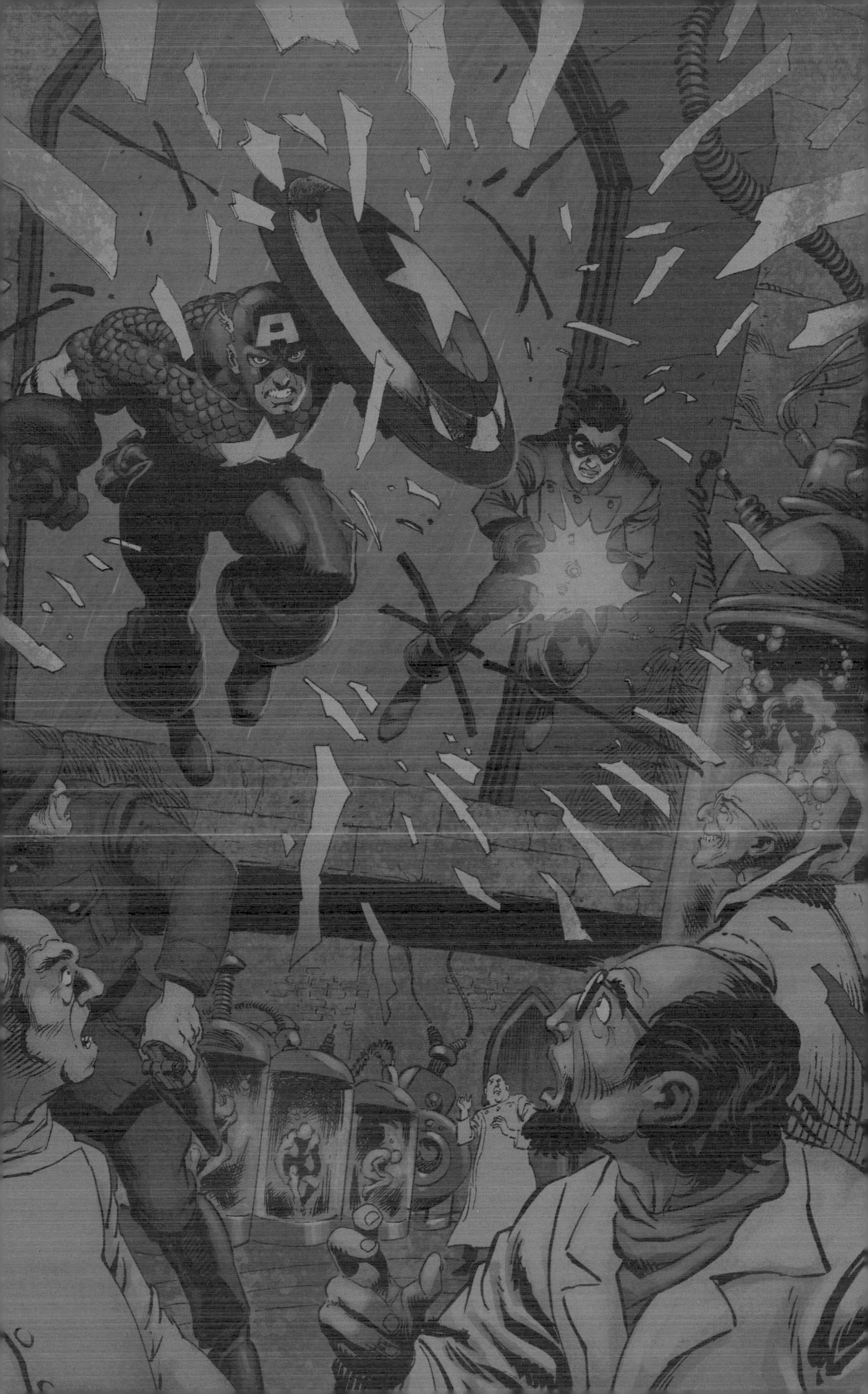

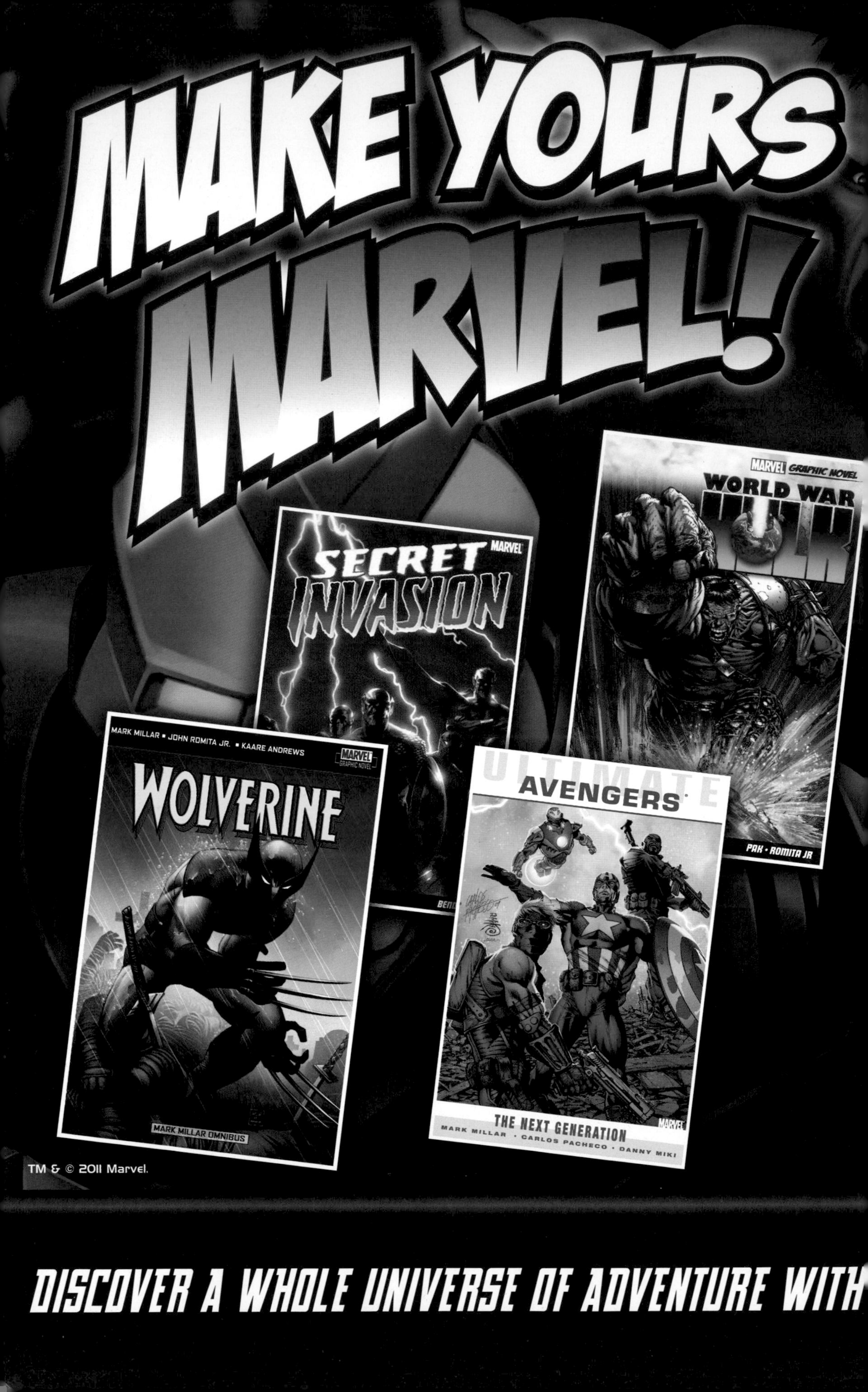
MAKE YOURS MARVEL!
SECRET INVASION
MARVEL
MARVEL GRAPHIC NOVEL
WORLD WAR HULK
PAK • ROMITA JR
MARK MILLAR • JOHN ROMITA JR. • KAARE ANDREWS
MARVEL GRAPHIC NOVEL
WOLVERINE
MARK MILLAR OMNIBUS
ULTIMATE
AVENGERS
THE NEXT GENERATION
MARVEL
MARK MILLAR • CARLOS PACHECO • DANNY MIKI
TM & © 2011 Marvel.
DISCOVER A WHOLE UNIVERSE OF ADVENTURE WITH

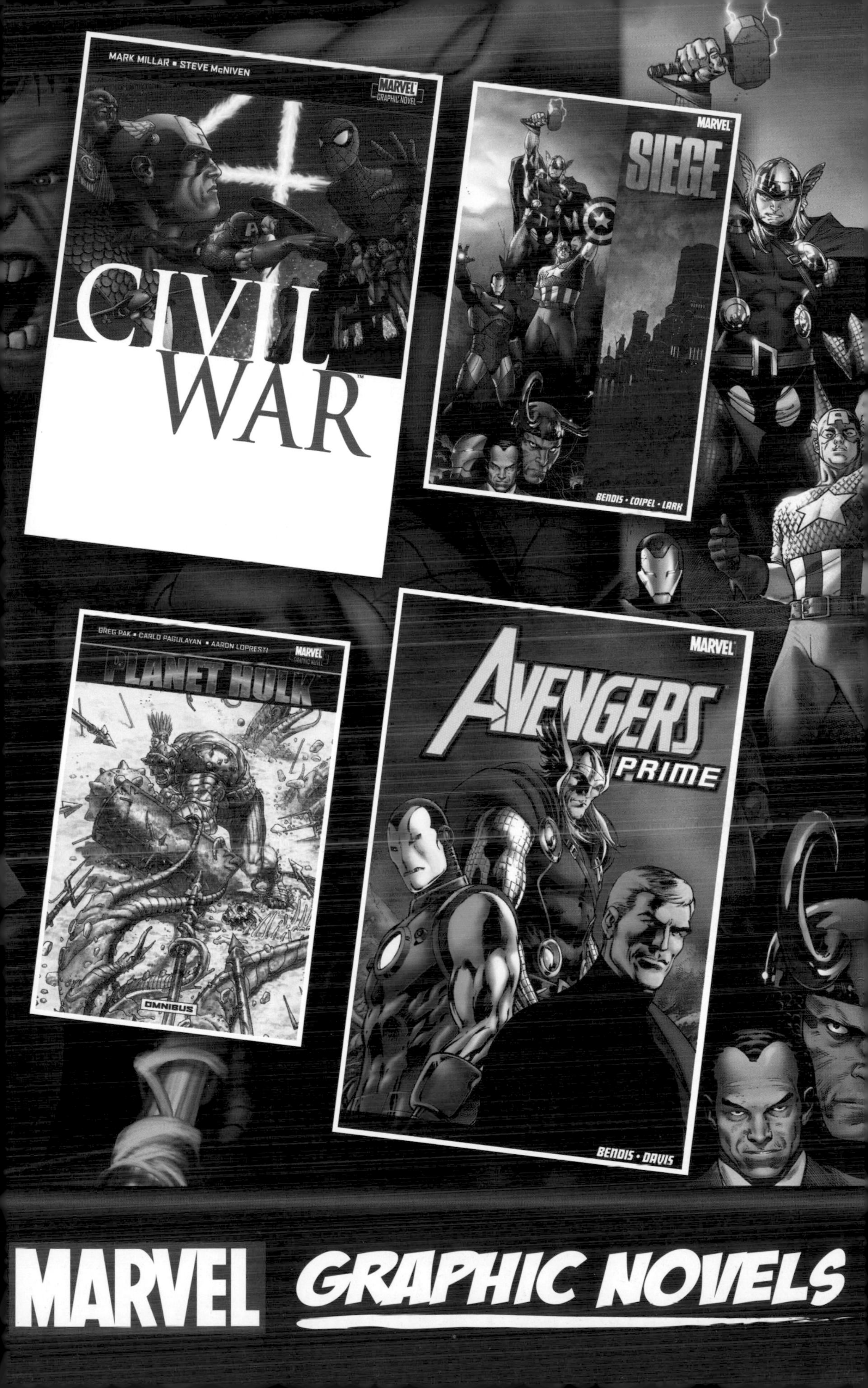
MARK MILLAR • STEVE McNIVEN
MARVEL GRAPHIC NOVEL
CIVIL WAR
MARVEL
SIEGE
BENDIS • COIPEL • LARK
GREG PAK • CARLO PAGULAYAN • AARON LOPRESTI
MARVEL GRAPHIC NOVEL
PLANET HULK
OMNIBUS
MARVEL
AVENGERS PRIME
BENDIS • DAVIS
MARVEL GRAPHIC NOVELS

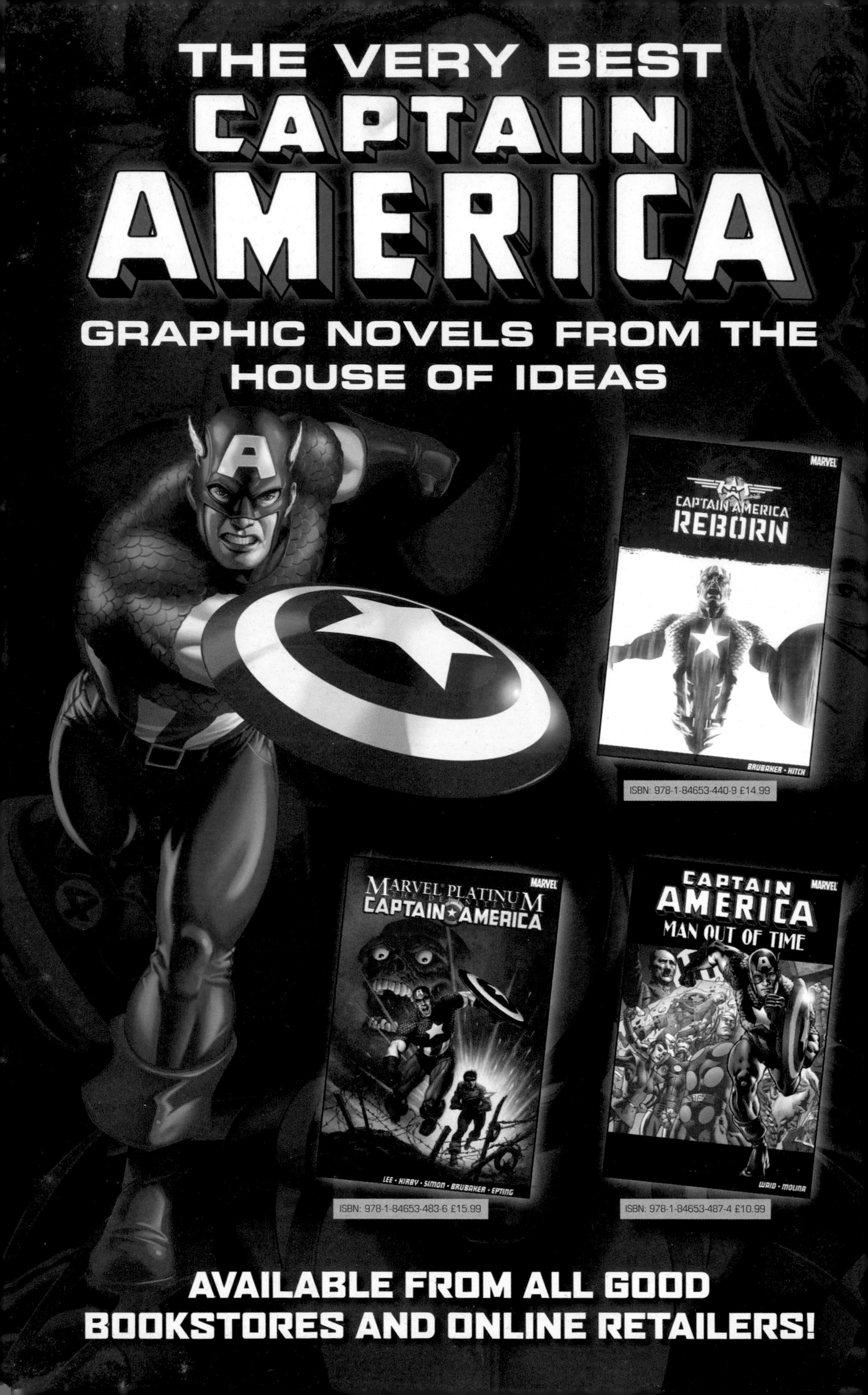
THE VERY BEST
CAPTAIN AMERICA
GRAPHIC NOVELS FROM THE HOUSE OF IDEAS
MARVEL
CAPTAIN AMERICA REBORN
BRUBAKER · HITCH
ISBN: 978-1-84653-440-9 £14.99
MARVEL
MARVEL PLATINUM THE DEFINITIVE CAPTAIN AMERICA
LEE · KIRBY · SIMON · BRUBAKER · EPTING
ISBN: 978-1-84653-483-6 £15.99
MARVEL
CAPTAIN AMERICA MAN OUT OF TIME
WAID · MOLINA
ISBN: 978-1-84653-487-4 £10.99
AVAILABLE FROM ALL GOOD BOOKSTORES AND ONLINE RETAILERS!